Chemistry
ADDISON-WESLEY

Small-Scale Chemistry
Laboratory Manual

EDWARD L. WATERMAN

Prentice Hall

Needham, Massachusetts
Upper Saddle River, New Jersey
Glenview, Illinois

Acknowledgments

Many people contributed ideas and resource during the development and writing of this small-scale laboratory manual. Mrs. Jackie Resseguie prepared solutions, organized equipment and provided other logistical support during the early stages of the experimental design. Peter Markow created the original formulation of the Thompson-Markow universal indicator and designed the first prototype of the small-scale balance which has since been modified and refined over the past decade by chemistry students at Rocky Mountain High School. These same students provided uncounted suggestions about the manuscript and numerous modifications of the experiments as they worked through them over the years. Bill Cook and Karen Dixon were enthusiastic cheerleaders at the appropriate moments. John Knight and Nicki Miller provided thoughts and insights as they worked through the experiments with their own students. The US West Foundation and the Hach Scientific Foundation provided resources to make the most of the time spent preparing the manuscript. Finally, a special thanks goes to Mrs. Kathryn C. Hach for her unparalleled love for and commitment to laboratory chemistry and the students who study it.

Cover photographs: Clockwise from top left: Test tube with zinc in acid, Richard Megma, Fundamental Photographs; Molecular structure of bucky ball, Ken Eward, Photo Researchers; Bunsen burner flame, and flask containing precipitate of lead(II) iodide, Richard Megma, Fundamental Photographs; Scanning tunneling microscope image, Fran Heyl Associates.

ISBN 0-13-054861-8

4 5 6 7 8 9 10   12 11 10 09 08 07 06

CONTENTS

TO THE STUDENT

Can you imagine learning how to play a musical instrument, paint a picture, or play a game by reading about it in a book? Books can give you valuable information when you are learning music, art, and sports, but to master any of these you have to practice and think about what you are doing as you are doing it.

The same is true of chemistry. The only way to really learn chemistry is to do chemistry. Chemistry is not a body of knowledge that exists in some textbook. Like music, art, and sports, it is something you do. To learn chemistry, you have to do lab work; you have to practice interacting with matter; you have to learn how to ask questions about matter, how to interpret the answers, and how to use this information to solve problems. Textbooks can be as valuable to chemistry students as they are to music students. But to learn the art of chemistry you have to participate in it.

This book is about practicing, or doing, chemistry. The idea is to put chemistry into your hands so you can explore chemistry for yourself. This book is designed to help you interact with matter, to interpret what you see, to solve problems, and to become inventive and creative. The labs are designed to help you to ask questions, to help you find ways to answer your questions, and to help you contribute your original ideas and discoveries to chemistry.

Practice chemistry yourself. Your participation will take patience. You will have to observe, concentrate, think about what you are doing, learn the rules, and apply the rules in original ways. If you do, you will discover that doing chemistry can be a lot of fun!

SMALL-SCALE LABORATORY SAFETY

The chemistry laboratory is a unique place where you will have the opportunity to investigate a variety of different chemical and physical phenomena. The experiments and procedures in this book have been carefully designed and written to minimize risk and provide for your personal safety. However, safety is also your responsibility. At all times your behavior is expected to be consistent with a safe laboratory. Here are some rules that are essential in promoting safety in the laboratory. You are responsible to know them and follow them at all times.

1. Wear safety glasses at all times when working in the laboratory or near someone else who is working in the laboratory. Safety glasses are designed to protect your eyes from injury due to chemicals and other foreign substances. To minimize the possibility of transmitting eye and skin disease, it's best to purchase and care for your own safety glasses. Do not loan them to another person. While working in the lab, do not rub your eyes because chemicals are easily transferred from your hands to your eyes.

2. Recognize that all laboratory procedures involve some degree of risk. Take steps to reduce the risk for yourself and for your neighbors. Read and listen to all directions carefully. When in doubt, ask your instructor.

3. Use full small-scale pipets only for the carefully controlled delivery of liquids, one drop at a time. Protect yourself and your neighbors by always using small-scale pipets correctly.

4. Minimize danger, waste, extra work, and cleanup by always using minimum amounts of chemicals to perform experiments.

5. Conduct only the assigned experiments, and do them only when a teacher is present and has given you permission to work.

6. Dispose of chemicals in a way that protects you, your neighbors, and your environment. Always follow your instructor's cleanup and disposal directions.

7. Know the location of the fire extinguisher, the emergency shower, the eye wash, the fire blanket, and the emergency exits. Know how and when to use each.

8. Consider all chemicals to be toxic. *Never* taste any laboratory chemical, including the many food products you will study in the laboratory. Consider these items to be contaminated with unknown chemicals. Keep all food and drink out of the laboratory. Do not eat, drink, or chew gum in the laboratory. Wash your hands thoroughly with soap and water before leaving the laboratory.

9. Report any accident, no matter how minor, to your instructor.

10. Recognize that electrical appliances pose an electrical shock hazard, especially in the presence of water. Keep electrical appliances away from sinks and faucets. Take care not to spill water or other liquids in the vicinity of an electrical appliance. If you do, stand back, notify your instructor, and warn other students in the area.

11. Do not handle heated glass or broken glass. In case of breakage, notify your instructor and your neighbors. Sweep up broken glass with a brush and pan provided by your instructor. Do not use chipped or cracked glassware. Discard it according to your instructor's directions.

12. Protect your clothing and hair from chemicals and sources of heat. Tie back long hair and roll up loose sleeves when working in the laboratory. Avoid wearing bulky or loose-fitting clothing. Remove dangling jewelry.

13. Wear closed-toed shoes in the laboratory at all times.

14. Help facilitate a quick exit from the classroom by keeping classroom furniture away from escape routes and walkways. Keep your work area orderly and free of personal belongings like coats and backpacks.

15. Safety begins and continues with a clean laboratory. Report chemical spills immediately to your instructor. Clean up spills according to your instructor's directions. Warn other students about the identity and location of spilled chemicals. Clean up thoroughly every time you finish your laboratory work.

16. Take appropriate precautions whenever any of the following safety symbols appear in an experiment.

 Eye Hazard
Wear safety goggles.

 Corrosive Substance Hazard
Wear safety goggles and laboratory apron.
Do not touch chemicals.

 Fire Hazard
Tie back hair and loose clothing.
Do not use a burner near flammable materials.

 Poison Hazard
Do not chew gum, drink, or eat in the laboratory.

Keep your hands away from your face.

 Electrical Hazard
Use care when using electrical equipment.

 Inhalation Hazard
Avoid inhaling this substance.

 Thermal Burn Hazard
Do not touch hot equipment.

 Breakage Hazard
Do not use chipped or cracked glassware.
Do not heat the bottom of a test tube.

 Disposal Hazard
Dispose of this chemical only as directed.

 Radiation Hazard
Use only calibrated and sealed sources.

Stapler

Alcohol thermometer

Scissors

Liquid soap dispenser

Office punch

Pipet rack

1 × 12

1 × 8

Well plates

Glass slide

Small-scale solid container/dispenser

Reagent bottle

Reagent-filling container

Plastic toothpick

Cotton swab

Small-scale spatula

Small-scale pipet

Small-scale weights

Cups

SMALL-SCALE EQUIPMENT

Cotton Swab: cotton and plastic; used to clean well plates, reaction surfaces.

Cups: plastic, 1-ounce and 31\2-ounces; used for titrations, balance pans, chromatography.

Glass Slide: only glass equipment in small-scale; may be heated used for evaporations.

Hot Plate: low-temperature capability, used for evaporations.

Liquid Soap Dispenser: plastic, used to wash hands after every laboratory.

Office Hole Punch, 1\4-inch: metal; used to punch holes in straws for construction of apparatus.

Pipet Rack: plastic; used to arrange and hold pipets for easy access.

Reagent Bottle: plastic; used to store solutions.

Reagent-Filling Container: plastic; used to fill pipets.

Safety Glasses: plastic; must be worn at all times while working in the laboratory.

Scissors: metal; used to cut papaer and plastic for construction of instruments.

Small-Scale Balance: student-built; used for quantitative chemistry.

Small-scale
reaction surface

Small-scale balance

Zipper-locking bag

Small-scale
spectroscope

Safety goggles

Small-scale
conductivity/electrolysis
device

Hot plate

Plastic spatula

Small-Scale Conductivity/Electrolysis Device: teacher- or stdudent-built; used to measure conductivity and to electrolyze solutions.

Small-Scale Pipet: plastic; used ot store and deliver liquids.

Small-Scale Reaction Surface: plastic; used to mix chemicals qualitatively.

Small-Scale Solid Container/Dispenser: plastic; used to store and dispense solids.

Small-Scale Spatula: student-built; used to sample solids.

Small-Scale Spectroscope: student-built; used for analysis of light.

Small -Scale Weights: student-built; used with balance to measure mass.

Spatula: plastic; used to retrieve hot glass slides from hot plate.

Stapler: metal and plastic; used in making weights, chromatogrphay, dispensing steel samples.

Thermometer: glass; alcohol type; used to measure temperature.

Toothpick: plastic; used to stir liquids in well plates.

Well Plates: plastic; common sizes are 1×12 and 1×8; used for quantitative work.

Zipper-Locking Bag: plastic; used to store weights and transfer dry-food samples.

SAFE AND EFFICIENT TECHNIQUES FOR USING SMALL-SCALE EQUIPMENT

This section will introduce you to some of the most commonly used pieces of small-scale equipment and give you tips on how to use them safely, efficiently, and without contamination. As you work your way through the experiments, you will want to refer to this information regularly. You are responsible for knowing these techniques and using them correctly!

Keep in mind that in the interest of safety, time, effort, and the environment, it's best to use only the amount of chemicals that you need. Small amounts of chemicals will do the same thing that larger amounts will do. The only difference is that small amounts are much safer, easier to clean up, and better for the environment.

The Small-Scale Pipet

The workhorse of the small-scale laboratory is the small-scale plastic pipet. Small-scale pipets serve two simultaneous functions: they store *and* dispense aqueous solutions of chemicals. Several pipets fit into the plastic pipet racks to make a convenient, readily available set of chemical solutions.

Preparing and Filling a Small-Scale Pipet

Most of the pipets you use in this course will be prepared for you. Your instructor might occasionally ask you to make and label your own. To do this, grasp a pipet firmly between your thumbs and forefingers at the center of the stem as shown in Figure I. Gently stretch the plastic stem so that it deforms to a smaller diameter. Cut the stem squarely with sharp scissors, leaving about 1 centimeter of the smaller stem as a tip.

Cut out a paper label and tape it to the pipet bulb so you can read it when the stem points up. Be sure to wrap the tape all the way around the bulb so that the tape overlaps itself and serves as a water-tight seal for the label.

To fill the pipet, wear your safety glasses and fill a reagent-filling container half full with reagent from a reagent bottle. Be sure to read the label! Point the tip of a pipet into an overturned plastic cup to prevent scattering stray droplets of liquid, and squeeze the bulb (Figure II). Now immerse the tip into the reagent-filling container and release the bulb. The pipet will fill with solution. To avoid contamination, do not return any unused solution to the reagent bottle. Replace the caps on both the reagent bottle and the reagent-filling container.

Small-scale pipets are easy to use, and the drop size they deliver makes handling them safe and efficient. They deliver drops having a volume of only about 20 microliters (20 millionths of a liter, or about 20 millionths of a quart). These small quantities of chemicals are also easier to clean up and present only a minimal environmental waste problem.

a. Grasp   **b.** Pull

c. Cut   **d.** Label

Figure I *Making and labeling a small-scale pipet*

a. Squeeze   **b.** Fill

Figure II *Filling a small-scale pipet*

The Small-Scale Reaction Surface

Rather than using conventional glassware like glass test tubes and beakers, you will carry out many of your experiments on a small-scale plastic reaction surface. Depending on what your teacher decides to use, this reaction surface might be a plastic file protector, and overhead projection transparency, or even a piece of plastic wrap. Your "reaction vessel" will be the drop of an aqueous solution that forms a hemispherical bead on the plastic surface. This bead is similar to the beads of water that form on a freshly waxed car. Because of surface tension, water naturally forms beads on plastic surfaces or on car wax. Water molecules have a relatively strong attraction for each other and no particular attraction for substances like plastic. A bead of water stays together because of this strong attraction. For this reason, the bead is an ideal reaciton vessel that you can use to carry out thousands of chemical reactions on a small scale. Because of its curved shape, the bead also serves as a magnifier. It enlarges the image of substances contained in the bead, making them easier to see.

The small-scale plastic surface encourages the use of smaller, safer, and more environmentally sound amounts of chemicals. An additional advantage of the reaction surface is that it allow for the placement of the directions and any special organization for an experiment in plain view, directly under the work surface. The reaction surface also allows for drops to appear on both white and black backgrounds.

Dispensing Drops from a Pipet onto a Reaction Surface

Full small-scale pipets are to be used only for the storage and carefully delivery of liquids. Delivering one drop at a time is the safest and most efficient use of the pipet. One-drop delivery is also the best way to avoid contamination. To deliver a drop, hold the pipet vertically over the reaction surface as in Figure III, so its tip is about 1 to 2 centimeters above the surface. The first drops sometimes contains an air bubble; if this is a problem, you may want to expel it into the sink or a waste cup before you begin. Never touch the tip of the pipet to the reaction surface. "Touching" drops onto the reaction surface causes contamination and makes it difficult to reproduce drops of the same size. Remember: Always *drop* the drops, never touch the drops onto the reaction surface.

a. Hold vertically   **b.** Squeeze gently   **c.** Allow drop to fall   **d.** Perfect

Stirring without Contamination

You can stir a hemispherical droplet on a reaction surface by gently blowing air from an empty pipet onto the droplet as in Figure IV, "air stirring." Aim the tip of an empty pipet at the droplet while holding it 2 to 3 centimeters away. Gently squeeze the bulb repeatedly. Moving air from the empty bulb will stir the contents of the droplet. Be sure not to touch the tip of the stirring pipet to the droplet as this will result in contamination, or the droplet might be absorbed into the stirring pipet. Both outcomes are undesirable.

a. Aim tip of empty pipet 2 to 3 cm away   **b.** Squeeze bulb gently; moving air stirs drop

Figure IV *Stirring a drop by blowing air from a small-scale pipet*

To correct errors on small parts of the reaction surface, simply absorb small amounts of any undesired material onto a cotton swab or onto the edge of a rolled paper towel as shown in Figure V.

a. With a cotton swab   **b.** With the edge of a rolled paper towel

Figure V *Correcting a mistake*

Cleaning the Small-Scale Reaction Surface

You can clean the small-scale reaction surface more quickly and easily than conventional glassware. To clean the entire reaction surface, absorb the liquids onto a paper towel and dispose the towel in a solid waste bin. Then wipe the surface with a damp paper towel. Finally, dry the surface with another paper towel. Take care that the chemical solutions touch only the paper towel and not your hands.

Disposal of paper towels is preferable to rinsing the chemicals down the drain because the paper towels eventually end up in landfills as solid waste. By contrast, liquid waste dumped down the drain ends up in sewage-treatment plants and can be introduced into rivers or lakes. Solid waste, while a mounting international problem, is much easier to control and to dispose of than liquid waste. Keeping solid waste to a minimum and disposing of it properly helps reduce environmental problems.

Plastic wrap as a reaction surface has the advantage that it does not need to be cleaned. When you are finished with it, simply fold it up carefully so that it contains all the chemicals you used, and dispose of it in the solid-waste bin. The disadvantage of plastic wrap is that its one time use and disposal requires that a lot of plastic be thrown away, a less than ideal or efficient use of resources! It is always better to clean, reuse, and recycle materials whenever you can.

Plastic Cups and Well Plates

Sometimes it will be more convenient to work on scales larger than just a few drops. You will use plastic cups and well plates for larger quantities. The balance pan, made from a plastic cup, is also a convenient large-reaction vessel. Water and water solutions bead up on plastic cups just as they do on reaction surfaces. You can stir the contents of a cup by gently swirling it. Most plastic cups have white insides, which serve as ideal built-in backgrounds for viewing chemical reactions. To clean a cup, rinse it with water, shake the water out, and dry it with a paper towel. To clean a well plate, flood it with water, and scrub the wells with a cotton swab. Shake the water out and dry the wells with a clean cotton swab. When you clean plastic cups and well plates, take care not to get the chemicals on your hands.

Dispensing Solids

To dispense solids into a cup or onto a reaction surface, simply remove the tape covering the hole in the top of the plastic vial and gently shake out the quantity you need. Alternatively, you can make a small-scale spatula by cutting a soda straw at an angle as shown in Figure VI. Use the straw to sample a portion of solid directly from the container. Your instructor will have lots of bits and pieces of recycled straws on hand for this purpose. Once a straw has been used with chemicals, do not use it again. Dispose of it according to your instructor's directions.

a. Cut at an angle   **b.** Two small-scale spatulas

Figure VI *Making a small-scale spatula from a soda straw*

The Safe Use of Glass Slides and Hot Plates

The glass microscope slide is one of the few pieces of glassware you will use in small-scale experiments. Before you use a glass slide, check to see that it is free of cracks and chips. Replace any broken slide with a new one. If you break a glass slide, notify your teacher. Sweep up the glass with a brush and pan. Never handle broken glass with your fingers!

From time to time it will be necessary to heat liquid droplets. The best way to heat droplets is to dispense them onto a glass slide and heat the slide on a hot plate. Because small-scale quantities require very little heat, usually the lowest setting on the hot plate is sufficient. Even so, keep in mind that the hot plate is hot, and so is the glass slide. A hot glass slide can burn you, and it will break if you drop it! Remove the hot slide using a plastic spatula. Even though the glass slide does not look hot, do not touch it until you have allowed it to cool on the lab bench. Do not place a hot slide on a plastic reaction surface; the thin plastic reaction surface will melt!

Keep in mind that hot plates are electrical appliances. To avoid electrical shock, keep them away from sinks, water faucets, and other sources of water.

Measuring Mass on a Small-Scale Balance

Early in this course you will construct your own small-scale balance. You will have the option of using it in a variety of experiments throughout the course to measure mass. Before you begin any weighing, check to see that the balance beam swings freely, without friction and interference. Use your small-scale balance to measure mass in the following ways:

1. To measure the mass of a solid object:

    a. Place the solid object in the pan.

    b. Adjust the beam and/or the counterweight so the beam rests in the horizontal position as indicated by the pointer. To check for accuracy, tap the beam gently so it oscillates back and forth without friction or interference and comes to rest in the horizontal position.

    c. Replace the object with known weights until the beam again returns to the horizontal position, oscillating freely and without interference.

2. To measure the mass of a specified amount of a liquid:

    a. Place a known mass equal in size to the mass of the liquid you wish to measure in the pan.

    b. Adjust the beam and/or the counterweight so the beam rests in the horizontal position as indicated by the pointer. To check for accuracy, tap the beam gently so it oscillates back and forth without friction or interference and comes to rest in the horizontal position.

    c. Remove the known weight and use a small-scale pipet to deliver, drop by drop, enough liquid to return the beam to the horizontal position, oscillating freely and without interference.

3. To calibrate a small-scale pipet:

    a. Place a 1000-mg mass in the pan.

    b. Adjust the beam and/or the counterweight so the beam rests in the horizontal position as indicated by the pointer. To check for accuracy, tap the beam gently so it oscillates back and forth without friction or interference and comes to rest in the horizontal position.

c. Remove the 1000-mg weight, and count from a small-scale pipet the number of drops needed to return the beam to the horizontal position. Divide 1000 by the number of drops to obtain the volume of a drop in microliters.

4. To measure the volume of a liquid delivered by a pipet:

a. Place a small-scale pipet full of the liquid you wish to deliver in the pan.

b. Adjust the beam and/or the counterweight so the beam rests in the horizontal position as indicated by the pointer. To check for accuracy, tap the beam gently so it oscillates back and forth without friction or interference and comes to rest in the horizontal position.

c. Deliver the required amount of liquid from the small-scale pipet to another container. Place the small-scale pipet back into the pan, and add enough known masses to return the beam to the horizontal position. The sum of the added masses is equal to the mass of the liquid you delivered to the container.

Measuring Mass on an Electronic Balance

As an alternative to the small-scale balance, your teacher may make an electonic balance available to you. Before proceeding with any weighing activity, push the tare control on the balance and wait for the digital display to stabilize at zero. Take care not to lean on the balance table or cause air currents to circulate about the balance. Place a clean, dry cup on the balance, push the tare control and wait for the digital display to stabilize at zero.

1. To measure the mass of a solid object:

a. Place the solid object in the cup and wait for the digital display to stabilize before you read the mass.

2. To measure the mass of a specified amount of liquid:

a. Remove the cup from the balance and carefully deliver liquid to the cup from a full small-scale pipet. A full pipet is approximately 4 g. Half a pipet is approximately 2 g.

b. Replace the cup on the balance pan and wait until the digital display stabilizes to read the mass. Keep in mind that for all the experiments you need not use the exact quantities of liquids specified. However, you do need to know what quantities you use.

3. To calibrate a small-scale pipet:

a. Remove the cup from the balance and holding a full small-scale pipet vertically, carefully deliver exactly 50 drops to the cup.

b. Replace the cup on the balance pan and wait for the digital display to stabilize before you read the mass. Divide the mass in milligrams by 50 to obtain the mass of a single drop in mg.

4. To measure the volume of a liquid delivered by a pipet:

a. Place a full small-scale pipet of the liquid you wish to deliver in the pan.

b. Deliver the required amount of liquid from the pipet to another container. Place the pipet back into the cup and wait for the digital display to stabilize before you read the weight.

Name _____ Class _____ Date _____

SAFETY CONTRACT

I have read in the Addison-Wesley *Small-Scale Chemistry Laboratory Manual* the pages that describe laboratory safety, laboratory hazards, and safe laboratory techniques. I have asked questions about any section that is unclear to me.

I agree to behave in a way that always promotes a safe laboratory environment for myself and my classmates. I agree to use chemicals and to clean them up in a way that protects myself, my classmates, and my environment.

I agree to wear safety glasses at all times during chemistry laboratory experiments and whenever my teacher thinks it is appropriate.

_____
Signature

_____
Date

1 A STUDY OF CHEMICAL CHANGES

Small-Scale Experiment for text section 2.4

OBJECTIVES

- **Observe** and **record** chemical changes involving chemicals found in common consumer products.
- **Design** and **carry out** experiments to identify chemicals in consumer products.
- **Demonstrate** the use of the names and formulas of common chemical compounds.

INTRODUCTION

Chemistry is a science that investigates changes in matter. Chemical reactions are the changes matter undergoes. The changes you can observe are called "macroscopic changes." Often these changes, such as color changes, the formation of a solid, or the formation of gas bubbles, are visible. Thus, though we can not see the atoms and molecules reacting, we can see indications that chemical changes have taken place.

Different atoms and molecules often react in different ways. Chemistry attempts to explain macroscopic changes in terms of the behavior of atoms and molecules, that is, on the submicroscopic level. You can use these different reactions to detect the presence of specific kinds of chemicals in mixtures.

PURPOSE

In this lab, you will study some reactions of common chemicals contained in consumer products. You will observe the notable macroscopic changes these chemicals undergo. In later labs, you will interpret these macroscopic changes in terms of submicroscopic changes, the behavior of atoms and molecules. As the name implies, submicroscopic changes are changes we cannot see, even with a microscope. The essence of understanding chemistry is to infer from macroscopic changes the submicroscopic behavior of atoms and molecules.

SAFETY

- Wear your safety glasses.
- Use full small-scale pipets only for the carefully controlled delivery of liquids.

MATERIALS

Small-scale pipets of the following solutions:

sodium hydrogen carbonate (NaHCO$_3$)	FD&C blue No. 1 (blue dye)
sodium hydrogen sulfate (NaHSO$_4$)	potassium iodide (KI)
phenolphthalein (phen)	calcium chloride (CaCl$_2$)
starch	sodium carbonate (Na$_2$CO$_3$)
ammonia (NH$_3$)	

sodium hypochlorite (NaOCl)
lead(II) nitrate (Pb(NO$_3$)$_2$)
silver nitrate (AgNO$_3$)
copper(II) sulfate (CuSO$_4$)
sodium hydroxide (NaOH)

hydrochloric acid (HCl)

EQUIPMENT

small-scale reaction surface   empty pipet for stirring

Name _____ Class _____ Date _____

EXPERIMENTAL DATA

Record your results in Table 1.1 or a table like it in your notebook.

Table 1.1   Experimental Mixings

a.	$NaHCO_3$ + HCl
b.	HCl + blue dye
c.	blue dye + NaOCl and then HCl
d.	NaOCl + KI and then starch
e.	KI + $Pb(NO_3)_2$
f.	$PB(NO_3)_2$ + $CaCl_2$
g.	$CaCl_2$ + $NaHSO_4$

h.	$NaHSO_4$ + Na_2CO_3
i.	Na_2CO_3 + phen
j.	phen + NaOH
k.	NaOH + $AgNO_3$
l.	$AgNO_3$ + NH_3
m.	NH_3 + $CuSO_4$
n.	$CuSO_4$ + $NaHCO_3$

CLEANING UP

Avoid contamination by cleaning up in a way that protects you and your environment. Carefully clean the small-scale reaction surface by absorbing the contents onto a paper towel, wipe it with a damp paper towel, and dry it. Dispose of the paper towels in the waste bin. Wash your hands thoroughly with soap and water.

QUESTIONS FOR ANALYSIS

Use what you learned in this lab to answer the following questions.

1. Sodium hydrogen carbonate is baking soda, $NaHCO_3$. When HCl is added to $NaHCO_3$, carbon dioxide bubbles are formed. Do you know the chemical formula of carbon dioxide? In what consumer product is the gas commonly found?

   _____

2. Which of the other mixings form bubbles?

   _____

3. What do you think the gas is that results from the mixing in Question 2?

   _____

4. The body uses hydrochloric acid, HCl, to help digest food. Where in the body is hydrochloric acid found? What color does blue food dye turn when HCl is added?

   _____

5. Sodium hypochlorite, NaOCl, is a common ingredient in household bleaches and cleansers. What happened to the color of blue dye when both HCl and NaOCl are added?

   _____

6. Potassium iodide, KI, is the source of iodine in iodized salt. What color is the KI + NaOCl mixture? What color does starch change to in the presence of KI and NaOCl?

   _____

7. A precipitate is a solid that separates upon mixing solutions. Which reaction produced a very bright yellow precipitate?

   _____

8. Which other mixings produced precipitates? Describe their colors and textures with words like milky, cloudy, and grainy.

   _____

9. Which mixture produced a precipitate that was very slow to form?

   _____

10. Which solutions produced a distinctive "muddy" brown precipitate?

    _____

11. Observe the scrap of paper you used to absorb the $AgNO_3$ + NH_3 mixture. What evidence do you see that indicates that silver compounds are light-sensitive?

    _____

12. Review your results and list at least three different kinds of changes that indicate that a chemical reaction is occurring.

_____

13. Describe any other notable observations you made.

_____

_____

NOW IT'S YOUR TURN!

1. What two compounds turn phenolphthalein pink in the original experiment? What others do this? Experiment and find out!

_____

_____

2. What happens when you add ammonia, NH_3, to copper(II) sulfate, $CuSO_4$? Does the result depend on the amount of ammonia you add? Try adding several drops of NH_3 to just 1 drop of $CuSO_4$. Then try adding several drops of $CuSO_4$. Record your observations.

_____

_____

_____

3. Sodium hydrogen carbonate, $NaHCO_3$, forms gas bubbles when hydrochloric acid, HCl, is added.

a. Suppose a label of a household product says it contains sodium hydrogen carbonate (also called bicarbonate of soda or baking soda). How would you test this material to indicate the presence of sodium hydrogen carbonate, $NaHCO_3$?

_____

_____

b. Try your procedure with various household products whose labels say they contain $NaHCO_3$. Record your results.

_____

c. Find out if any of the other chemicals you used in this experiment form gas bubbles with hydrochloric acid. Based on your results, describe any limitations this experiment might have.

_____

_____

_____

_____

4. Many foods contain starch. You know that starch turns black in the presence of potassium iodide, KI, and sodium hypochlorite, NaOCl. Try adding KI and NaOCl to various foods to confirm the presence or absence of starch. Explain what you do, what you observe, and what it means.

_____

_____

_____

5. Potassium iodide, KI, turns black when sodium hypochlorite, NaOCl, and starch are added. The label on a package of iodized table salt says that it contains potassium iodide, KI. Tell what you would do to confirm this. Try it and record your results. Does your procedure work with non-iodized salt? Explain.

_____

_____

_____

_____

_____

6. Many household products like automatic dishwashing liquid contain sodium hypochlorite, NaOCl. Design an experiment to confirm the presence or absence of NaOCl in automatic dishwashing liquid and other household chemicals. Add one drop of starch and one drop of KI to the household chemical which lists NaOCl as an ingredient. A black color confirms the presence of NaOCl. Note: Do not use full strength household bleach. Dilute 50 mL of household bleach with 200 mL of water.

2 DESIGN AND CONSTRUCTION OF A SMALL-SCALE BALANCE

Small-Scale Experiment for text section 3.1

OBJECTIVES

- **Design** and **build** a balance that is capable of accurately weighing 10 grams and is sensitive to 5 milligrams.

- **Explain** the relationship between the structure and function of each part of a balance.

- **Troubleshoot** the balance, and make modifications and innovations to make it work better.

INTRODUCTION

A *balance* is an instrument used to measure mass. Because it is often the most accurate instrument in the laboratory, you commonly use the balance to calibrate other instruments, such as burets and pipets, that are used to measure volume. The balance operates much like a see-saw because it consists of a *beam* that pivots on a central *fulcrum* as shown in Figure 2.1. A *balance pan* hangs from one end of the beam, and a *counterweight* is attached to the other end. You use a *substitution balance* to determine mass by comparing the weight of an unknown object to the weights of known objects. You place a substance of unknown weight in the pan and adjust the mechanism so the beam balances. You then remove the unknown substance and substitute known weights until the beam balances again. The weight of the unknown substance is equal to the amount of known weights you used to restore the beam to the balanced position.

Sensitivity refers to the smallest weight a balance can measure accurately. Whenever you add weight to the pan, the balance beam moves. You express the sensitivity of the balance as the amount of change in the position of the beam when a known quantity of weight is added. Sensitivity can be measured by the *distance* the beam moves or the *angle* through which the beam moves per unit weight. The smaller the weights you want to measure accurately, the more sensitive your balance must be. If the balance is too sensitive, it will move with even the slightest air currents and will be difficult to use.

The *capacity* of a balance is the maximum amount of weight that can be accurately determined by the balance. Very sensitive balances generally have small capacities. With larger-capacity balances, you sacrifice sensitivity. You want a balance to be just sensitive enough to do the job in a convenient way. You design a balance to make the best compromise among sensitivity, capacity, and ease of use.

The principal moving part of the balance is the *beam*. The beam's mass, length, and flexibility affect the sensitivity of the balance. The longer, lighter, and more rigid the beam, the more sensitive the balance will be. However, the longer the beam, the heavier it is. In designing your beam, find a compromise between the extremes of length and mass, and yet design it to remain rigid under maximum loads. Very sensitive balances have the advantage of measuring the masses of very small objects accurately. Unfortunately, they cannot weigh heavy objects because the long light beam required for high sensitivity is usually too flexible to carry large loads. Balances designed to weigh larger objects must use rigid beams, which are usually very heavy. Thus, sensitivity is sacrificed for capacity and vice versa. In short, the same balance cannot be used to weigh both a truck and a feather. Designers of balances must make compromises and design balances that meet specific objectives. You want your balance to be sensitive to 5 milligrams and have a capacity of about 10 grams.

Figure 2.1 *Construction of a small-scale balance*

The most critical part of the balance is the *fulcrum*, the part on which the beam pivots. For maximum sensitivity, the fulcrum should be nearly friction-free. You should locate it above and at right angles to the beam, and as close to the beam's center of mass as possible. The beam will swing freely back and forth only if the center of mass of the beam is *below* the fulcrum. The beam will not be stable if the center of gravity is above the fulcrum.

A highly visible *pointer* readily determines the horizontal position of the beam. The balance is most sensitive when the beam is exactly horizontal. The pointer should be attached rigidly and at right angles to the beam and the fulcrum. When the beam is horizontal, the pointer will be vertical.

The *zero point* is the point indicated by the pointer when the beam is horizontal. In order to know the horizontal position reliably, the zero point must not move from one weighing to another.

The *balance posts* and *crossmember* make up the superstructure that gives support and stability to the balance and does not interfere with its operation. The balance posts must be anchored and rigid because if they move, the zero point moves. Build the posts perpendicular to the base, then center the zero point in a fixed position between the posts. With a sharp pencil, make holes in the straw posts to provide nearly frictionless surfaces to support the fulcrum. The taller the posts and the longer the pointer, the easier it is to see a small movement in the beam. However, very tall posts are sometimes not rigid enough to support the weight of the instrument.

The *pan pivot* suspends the pan from the beam. Like the fulcrum, it must be sturdy, nearly frictionless, and at right angles to the beam. The pan pivot must not move back and forth along the beam.

The *balance pan* holds the known weights and the objects you want to weigh. The balance pan should be sturdy and lightweight to keep the beam's center of mass close to the fulcrum.

The *beam stops* hit the pointer and allow the beam to move only through a small arc. By preventing excessive motion of the balance beam, they protect the vital moving parts of the balance and shorten the time the beam takes to come to the horizontal position. The sensitivity of a good balance is such that even the slightest touch will cause the balance beam, without beam stops, to rotate and the pan to swing wildly. When trying to make an accurate weighing, this situation is inconvenient at best and disastrous at worst.

The *counterweight* offsets the weight in the pan. A friction-tight but easily moved counterweight serves as a convenient adjustment device for leveling the beam. Make it light to keep the total weight of the beam assembly low.

Summary of principal parts of a balance and their functions:

- A *balance* is an instrument used to measure mass.

- The *beam* is the principal moving part. The beam also affects sensitivity. For maximum sensitivity, it should be lightweight, rigid, and long.

- The *fulcrum* is the critical pivot point for the beam. The position and friction of the fulcrum affect accuracy and sensitivity. The fulcrum should be frictionless at the posts, friction-tight at the pointer, close to the beam's center of mass and just above it, and at right angles to the beam and the posts.

- The *counterweight* moves to offset the weight in the pan. The counterweight is light and friction-tight but easily moved.

- *Sensitivity* refers to the smallest weight a balance can measure accurately.

- The *capacity* of a balance is the maximum amount of weight that can be accurately determined by the balance.

- The *pointer* points to the zero point when the beam is horizontal. The pointer should be long, visible, and at right angles to the beam.

- The *zero point* shows when the beam is horizontal. The zero point is positioned so the pointer points to it when the beam is horizontal.

- The *posts* support the weight of the balance. They should be sturdy, friction-tight, and out of the way of moving parts.

- The *crossmember* keeps the balance rigid and square. The crossmember is friction-tight and at right angles to the posts.

- The *pan pivot* is the critical point upon which the pan rests. The pan pivot is frictionless at the beam, at right angles to the beam, and foolproof so the pan does not fall off.

- The *beam stops* keep the beam from swinging wildly. The beam stops are sturdy and out of the way of moving parts.

PURPOSE

In this lab you will design and construct a balance out of common objects such as soda straws, pins, tape, wood blocks, wire, and plastic cups. For optimal use in small-scale chemistry, your balance should be sensitive to 5 milligrams and have a capacity of 10 grams. Your balance should be sturdy and foolproof so it can make many accurate weighings in very short times with little trouble. You should build your balance with careful consideration of features that make it function accurately and reliably. The preceding paragraphs provided information about the working parts of a balance. Reread them and refer to these criteria as you design and build your balance.

SAFETY

- Behave in a way that is consistent with a safe laboratory.

EQUIPMENT

6 soda straws	1 pre-drilled wood block
1 extra long pin (1-1/4 inch)	4 square centimeters of graph paper
2 paper clips	1 plastic cup
1 adhesive label	scissors
thread	cellophane tape
wire	longer soda straws
1/4-inch office hole punches	standard 5 mg weights

EXPERIMENTAL PROCEDURE

Use the following template to assemble the proper pieces for constructing your small-scale balance. Use the template to cut the soda straws to the appropriate lengths. Use a 1/4-inch office hole punch to make holes where indicated. Use a sharp pencil to make holes in the posts for the fulcrum. Assemble the parts as shown in the template and in Figure 2.1.

Name _____ Class _____ Date _____

EXPERIMENTAL DATA

As you assemble your balance according to the template on the Experimental Page, check it and make adjustments and/or modifications until the answer to each of the following questions is "yes."

_____   1. Is the fulcrum perpendicular to both the beam and the pointer?

_____   2. Is it just *above* and *touching* the beam?

_____   3. Does the fulcrum rotate freely from the holes in the post?

_____   4. Are the holes round and large enough to allow a pin head to pass through?

_____   5. Is the fulcrum friction-tight at the pointer?

_____   6. Is the pin straight?

_____   7. Are the posts friction-tight at the base?

_____   8. Is the crossmember friction-tight?

_____   9. Are the posts and crossmember rigid and out of the way of the moving parts?

_____   10. Do the beam stops keep the beam from swinging excessively?

_____   11. Are the beam stops out of the way of all other moving parts?

_____   12. Does the pan stay on consistently?

_____   13. Is the pan easily loaded with weight?

_____   14. Does the pan pivot at right angles to the beam?

_____   15. Does the beam not bend under weight?

_____   16. Is the end of the pointer easy to see?

_____   17. Does the pointer point at the zero point when the beam is horizontal?

_____   18. Is the zero point positioned to indicate when the beam is horizontal?

_____   19. Is the pointer at right angles to the beam?

_____   20. Is the counterweight easily moved but friction-tight to stay in place?

_____   21. Can you easily fix anything that goes wrong with your balance?

_____   22. Does the pointer move when a 15-milligram weight is placed on the pan?

_____   A 10-milligram weight?

_____   A 5-milligram weight?

_____   The *sensitivity* of the balance is the minimum weight on the pan that will cause the pointer to move. Each of the three weights cause the beam to move how many graph-paper units?

Name _____ Class _____ Date _____

CLEANING UP

Please clean up at the end of the period. Recycle all the materials you do not use. Dispose of unusable scraps in the waste bin. Label your balance with your name, and store it as directed by your teacher.

QUESTIONS FOR ANALYSIS

Use what you learned in this lab to answer the following questions.

1. How does a substitution balance work? Does it measure mass or weight? Explain. Make a rough sketch of your balance and label all the parts.

   _____

   _____

   _____

   _____

   _____

   _____

2. What is sensitivity? What is capacity?

   _____

   _____

3. What critical part of a balance most affects its sensitivity? Give three important criteria for this critical part.

   _____

   _____

4. Name another part of a balance that also affects its sensitivity.

   _____

5. At what position is the beam most sensitive?

   _____

6. What is the function of the pointer? Of the zero point?

   _____

7. Why is it important for the balance posts and crossmember to be well-anchored and rigid?

   _____

8. What aspects of your balance are most important?

   _____

Design and Construction of a Small-Scale Balance **31**

9. What other criterion besides sensitivity must be considered when creating a balance beam?

_____

10. Explain how each of the following materials would affect the *sensitivity* and *capacity* of your balance if each material was used for the beam. Give the advantages and disadvantages of each: **a.** a solid steel rod, **b.** a hollow aluminum tube, and **c.** a wood dowel.

_____

_____

11. The sensitivity of a balance increases with increasing length and decreasing mass of the beam. Why is the ideal case of having an infinitely long beam of zero mass not possible?

_____

12. How many graph-paper units did the pointer move upon addition of a 10-mg weight? Explain how you might make your balance even more sensitive.

_____

13. Why is it important to have the holes in which the fulcrum rest at exactly the same height? If they are not at the same height, how might you be able to fix them without remaking one or both the posts?

_____

_____

14. If the fulcrum pin were placed at a 45-degree angle to the beam, how would this affect the function and sensitivity of your balance?

_____

_____

_____

NOW IT'S YOUR TURN

1. Why must the fulcrum be placed *above the beam*? What will happen to a balance beam set in motion if the fulcrum is below it? (To answer these questions, see what happens when you place the fulcrum below the beam. Go ahead; you can always move it back!)

_____

_____

2. Design a longer beam for your balance. Use a 1/4-inch wood dowel, an aluminum tube, and an extra-long soda straw, or try to put together one or more soda straws. What are some of the advantages and disadvantages of your longer beam?

3. Design a better way to hold your balance up. Redesign the posts into a more rigid superstructure. Try building a triangular or a rectangular superstructure.

4. A taller balance will be more sensitive because the movement of a long pointer will be easier to detect for a small weight. Try modifying your balance so that it is very tall.

5. Try redesigning the beam-fulcrum assembly. You might consider using permanent magnets to suspend the beam-fulcrum.

3 DESIGN AND CONSTRUCTION OF A SET OF STANDARDIZED WEIGHTS

Small-Scale Experiment for text section 3.3

OBJECTIVES

- **Distinguish** between mass and weight.
- **Construct** a set of weights to use with a small-scale balance.
- **Weigh** objects accurately using your weights.

INTRODUCTION

Now that you've built a balance, you can use it to measure mass. To do so, you must first make a set of known weights to use with your balance for comparison with unknown weights. But before you make the weights, let's clarify a few things about how mass is different from weight.

Mass is the quantity of matter in an object. *Weight*, on the other hand, is the gravitational force of attraction exerted between the mass of an object and its surroundings, principally the earth. The weight of an object on Earth will differ slightly depending on its geographical location. Because the gravitational field is weaker at the equator than at the poles, the same object will weigh less in Mexico City than in Anchorage, Alaska. The gravitational pull also decreases with higher elevation. An object will weigh slightly less in Denver, "the mile-high city," than in New York, which is at sea level.

In chemistry you are always interested in the determination of mass because you do not want the results to depend on where you are. You can readily determine mass by comparing the weight of an unknown object to the weights of known objects through the use of a *balance*, a device used to compare weights. Since gravity will affect both known and unknown objects to exactly the same extent, the effect of gravity will cancel, and a measure of mass will result.

It is important to note that the distinction between mass and weight in chemistry is not commonly observed. For example, determining the mass of an object is called *weighing*. Known masses that are used to compare unknown masses are called *weights*. Hereafter, we will use the terms *mass* and *weight* synonymously, but strictly speaking, we are referring to *mass*.

To weigh things accurately, your small-scale balance is used with a set of weights. The set of weights must be calibrated, that is, compared to accurately known weights. Calibration is usually done with a balance more sensitive and accurate than your small-scale balance. Once calibrated, this known set of weights will become your set of standardized weights.

The number and sizes of standardized weights in a set should be such that any combination of weight can be added within the sensitivity and capacity of the balance. Your balance has a sensitivity of 5 mg and a capacity of about 10 g (10 000 mg). Thus, you need to build a set of weights that can combine to provide any number of milligrams between 5 mg and 10 000 mg in intervals of 5 milligrams.

PURPOSE

In this lab, you will take advantage of small objects that can be uniformly reproduced to make a set of standardized weights. Common objects like staples, soda straws, graph paper, and wire all have reproducible weights for equal-sized pieces. The plastic "disks" punched from super-jumbo soda straws all weigh exactly 5 mg. Standard staples all weigh 33 mg, and graph paper, if cut precisely, can produce very uniform small weights. Large objects are not as uniformly produced, but they can be standardized by weighing them and labeling them with their milligram values.

SAFETY

- Behave in a way that is consistent with a safe laboratory.

EQUIPMENT

1/2 page of graph paper
1 standard paper clip
1 jumbo paper clip
1 zipper-locking plastic sandwich bag
1 penny
1 nickel
staplers with standard staples
1/4-inch office hole punches
soda straws
adhesive labels
scissors

EXPERIMENTAL PROCEDURE

Use the information below to design a set of weights, and then make them with the available materials. Where you can, write the weight value and your name on each weight. Place them in a labeled zipper-locking sandwich bag for storage.

Weights with the following milligram values will enable you to weigh any object between 5 mg and 10 000 mg. Your set of weights will probably not be ideal; that is, some of the values will not be exactly the values listed below.

5 mg	10 mg	20 mg	30 mg
50 mg	100 mg	200 mg	300 mg
500 mg	1000 mg	2500 mg	5000 mg

1. One 1/4-inch plastic disk cut from a soda straw weighs 5 mg. Make enough plastic disks to weigh things between 5 and 45 mg.

2. Design and make weights from 50 to 500 mg, using the following information:
    1 square inch of graph paper (cut very carefully) weighs 50 mg.
    1 standard staple weighs 33 mg.

    Keep in mind that the staples tend to be more precise than the graph paper, and the weights need to be within only a few (2 to 3) milligrams of the ideal values.

3. Make the following larger weights, and then use your small-scale balance and your smaller weights to determine their masses.

   1 standard paper clip with an adhesive label attached.
   1 jumbo paper clip with an adhesive label attached.
   1 penny with an adhesive label attached.
   1 nickel with an adhesive label attached.

   To use your balance to determine the mass of a larger weight, follow these steps:

   a. Place the larger weight in the pan, and slide the beam and/or the counterweight back and forth so the pointer indicates the beam is horizontal.

   b. Remove the larger weight from the pan, and replace it with smaller weights until the pointer again indicates the beam is horizontal.

   c. The weight of the larger weight is the sum of the small weights in the pan.

   d. Write this milligram value on the label of the larger weight.

4. If your lab has a precision or analytical balance, use it to check the weights of your larger weights, following the directions of your teacher. Also, in the next lab you will do some experiments to find out how good your weights really are!

EXPERIMENTAL DATA

1. Draw a picture of each standardized weight you make, tell what it is made from, and label it with its milligram value.

 $\frac{1}{4}$-inch disk cut from straw-5 mg

50 mg-1 square inch
graph paper

5083 mg

nickel with
adhesive label

525 mg

standard paper clip
with adhesive label

standard staples

100 mg

300 mg

1610 mg

jumbo paper clip
with adhesive label

200 mg

500 mg

2550 mg

penny with
adhesive label

CLEANING UP

Please recycle all the materials you do not use. Dispose of unusable scraps in the waste bin. Store your labeled weights as directed by your teacher.

QUESTIONS FOR ANALYSIS

Use what you learned in this lab to answer the following questions.

1. Distinguish between the terms *mass* and *weight*. Why do we often use them interchangeably?

_____

_____

_____

2. What is the mass of an object in outer space, where there is no gravitational field? What is its weight?

_____

Name _____ Class _____ Date _____

3. Will the mass of an object be the same on Earth as it is on the moon? Explain.

   _____

   _____

4. Is the weight of an object the same on Earth as it is on the moon? Explain.

   _____

   _____

5. Would your balance work equally well on the moon as it does on Earth? Explain.
   Would the result of each weighing be the same? Explain.

   _____

   _____

   _____

6. Would your balance work equally well in the absence of a gravitational field, say,
   in outer space? Explain.

   _____

7. Explain what we mean by the *sensitivity* and *capacity* of a balance.

   _____

   _____

8. Your balance is sensitive to 5 mg, and its capacity is about 10 g, or 10 000 mg. Are
   the weights you made sufficient to measure any unknown weight up to 10 000 mg
   to a sensitivity of 5 mg?

   _____

   _____

9. The mass of a carbon atom is about 2.0×10^{-23} g. Discuss the major problems
   associated with determining the mass of a carbon atom by using a balance of the
   design you have constructed.

   _____

   _____

   _____

   _____

10. If you weigh an object in Panama and again in Canada on the same balance, will
    you get the same value for its weight? Explain.

    _____

    _____

11. Which of the following would be useful in studying the small differences in gravitational field in various locations: a balance or a spring scale that measures weight? Explain.

_____

NOW IT'S YOUR TURN!

1. Can you devise another way to make small-scale weights? If your laboratory has a precision or analytical balance, you may want to use it to investigate the weights of various common objects to see if you can devise a better set of standardized weights.

2. If your lab does have a very sensitive balance, you can make larger weights from a standardized spool of brass or steel wire. Since wire is very uniform, its length is proportional to its weight. All you need to know is how much a certain length of wire weighs, and you can make any size weight you want by measuring the appropriate length. Notice that you are basing mass on the fundamental quantity of length. By using a very sensitive and accurate analytical balance, you can determine what the mass of one meter of any wire is. From this you can calculate what length of wire must be cut to make a weight of any desired quantity. Typical results might look something like this:

to make a wire of this *weight* (mg)	cut a wire to this *length* (cm)
500.0	53.4
300.0	32.0
200.0	21.3
100.0	10.7
50.0	5.34
30.0	3.20
20.0	2.13
10.0	1.07
5.0	0.534

Each spool of wire is slightly different in weight, so each must be calibrated and a table of weights made accordingly. Also, the smaller weights (100 mg and smaller) are often difficult to store and handle, so it is less convenient to make these smaller weights from wire.

Beginning with the largest weight measure, cut the indicated length of wire by stretching it along a meter stick, smoothing out any bends and kinks as you go. Keep in mind that wire is ductile; it will become longer if stretched too hard. The trick is to smooth out the bends and kinks while handling the wire gently.

To store the larger wire weights, you can wrap the wire in a tight coil around a nail and poke one end into a straw on the beam stop. You should mark each one to distinguish it from other weights.

4 WEIGHING ACTIVITIES FOR A SMALL-SCALE BALANCE

Small-Scale Experiment for text section 4.3

OBJECTIVES

- **Determine** accurate weights of various objects by using a small-scale balance.
- **Calibrate** a pipet by weighing drops.

INTRODUCTION

How accurate are your weights? How well does your balance work? Will it help you get the right answers? What is a "right answer," anyway? Now that you've spent so much time building your balance and weights, what kinds of problems can you solve with them?

PURPOSE

In this lab you will explore a few of these questions. You will begin by tuning your balance and set of weights by using them to weigh objects of known mass. You will compare your results to the known values to evaluate how good your balance is. Then you will make any necessary adjustments and explore ways you can use your balance to investigate matter, answer questions, and solve problems.

The first thing you will do is weigh a penny and compare it to its known weight. If your result is not close, you will make the necessary adjustments to your balance and/or weights and try again until you can consistently weigh known objects to a high degree of accuracy. Then you can rely on your balance and use it to find unknown masses.

SAFETY

- Behave in a way that is consistent with a safe laboratory.

EQUIPMENT

various objects to weigh, like pennies, nickels, and dimes
adhesive labels
small-scale balance
small-scale pipet filled with water

EXPERIMENTAL PROCEDURE

Part A. Weighing Pennies

1. Place a small adhesive label on a penny and weigh the penny as follows. Record your results in Table 4.1.

   a. Place the penny in the balance pan, and move the beam and the counterweight until the pointer indicates the beam is horizontal.

   b. Remove the penny and substitute weights until the pointer is again zeroed. If you go too far, do not be afraid to remove a larger weight and replace it with a smaller one.

   c. When you think the beam is horizontal, tap the beam gently and allow it to make a few oscillations before coming to rest. This avoids a false rest point due to friction at the fulcrum.

   d. The weight of the penny in milligrams is the sum of the weights in the pan. Calculate the *absolute error* and *percent relative error* of the penny weighed on your small-scale balance compared to the same penny weighed on an electronic balance as follows: (Assume that the electronic weight is the actual or theoretical weight.)

   $$\text{absolute error} = |\text{small-scale weight} - \text{electronic weight}|$$

   $$\% \text{ relative error} = \frac{|\text{small-scale weight} - \text{electronic weight}|}{\text{electronic weight}} \times 100$$

2. Weigh a second penny (with a label) and calculate its percent relative error. Record your results in Table 4.1. If the absolute error in the case of either penny is greater than about 10 mg, and the percent relative error is greater than about 0.5% error, work with your balance and your weights to determine the cause. Obtain another penny, and repeat Part A until you can weigh a penny to within a 0.5% error. Label this penny with your name and its weight in milligrams, and keep it as a standard weight. Hints: The most common problem is friction at the fulcrum. Adjust your balance so the beam assembly moves freely. Also ask your instructor to weigh your larger weights for you to determine if they are accurate.

Part B. Weighing Experiments

3. Weigh a nickel and calculate its absolute, relative, and percent error. Record your results in Table 4.1. Label your nickel as you labeled your penny, and keep it as a standard weight.

4. Weigh a dime and calculate its absolute, relative, and percent error. Record your results in Table 4.1.

5. Design an experiment to find the weight in milligrams of 1 drop of water. Record your results in Table 4.2. Count the number of drops it takes to equal a certain weight. (Any weight will do!) Divide that weight by the number of drops to get the weight of a drop. Repeat the experiment with various sizes of weights to see how consistent you can be. Try 100, 300, 500, and 1000 mg weights.

6. Design an experiment to determine if the size of drops varies with the angle at which they are delivered. Record your results in Table 4.3. Use a 1000 mg weight. Try vertical (90°), horizontal (0°), and halfway between (45°).

Name _____ Class _____ Date _____

EXPERIMENTAL DATA

Record your results in Tables 4.1, 4.2, and 4.3 or tables like them in your notebook.

Table 4.1   Weighing Coinage

Object	Small-Scale Weight (mg)	Electronic Weight (mg)	Absolute Error (mg)	Percent Error
penny #1				
penny #2				
nickel				
dime				

Table 4.2   Weighing a Drop of Water

Weight (mg)	Number of Drops	Weight of Drops (mg)
100		
300		
500		
1000		

Table 4.3   Checking Drop Angle

Drop Angle	Number of Drops	Weight of Drop (mg)
vertical (90°)		
horizontal (0°)		
halfway (45°)		

CLEANING UP

Please recycle all the materials you do not use. Store your balance and weights according to your teacher's directions.

QUESTIONS FOR ANALYSIS

Use what you learned in this lab to answer the following questions.

1. Discuss some major sources of error if a weighing has a percent relative error of greater than about 0.5%.

   _____

   _____

2. If your weighings exceed about 0.5% relative error, what changes might you make to get better results?

   _____

   _____

3. How many milligrams does 1 drop of water weigh?

   _____

4. How many grams does 1 drop of water weigh? (1000 mg = 1 g.)

$$x \text{ g} = 1 \text{ drop} \times \frac{\text{wt. of drops (mg)}}{\text{no. of drops}} \times \frac{1 \text{ g}}{1000 \text{ mg}} =$$

5. If you use a larger weight to determine the size of a drop, will you get a more or less accurate result than with a smaller weight? Explain.

   _____

6. What angle for holding the pipet is best? Explain. Why is it important to expel the air bubble before you begin the experiment?

   _____

   _____

   _____

7. What is the volume in cm^3 of 1 drop? The density of water is 1.00 g/cm^3. This means that 1 gram of water occupies a volume of 1 cubic centimeter. Thus, if we measure weight, we can calculate volume as a function of weight. That is, if we weigh a certain amount of water, we will know its volume.

$$x \text{ cm}^3 = 1 \text{ drop} \times \frac{\text{no. of grams}}{1 \text{ drop}} \times \frac{1 \text{ cm}^3}{1 \text{ g}} =$$

Calculate the volume of a single drop in mL. (1 mL = 1 cm^3.) What is the volume of a drop in microliters, µL? (1000 mL = 1 µL.)

   _____

8. What is the density of water in units of mg per cm^3? (1 gram = 1000 mg.) Express the density in units of mg per mL.

_____

NOW IT'S YOUR TURN!

1. Recently, the United States government changed the composition of the American penny, which had remained essentially the same for nearly 120 years. Older pennies are made of an alloy consisting of 95% copper and 5% zinc. The newer penny's copper coating comprises only 2.4% of its total weight. This copper-coated zinc slug looks just like its copper ancestor, but it is easily distinguished by its different weight. Because the density of zinc is less than that of copper, the newer pennies are lighter than the older ones.

Obtain a set of ten pennies dated 1978–1987 from your teacher. Use your balance to determine in which year the penny's composition changed. Hint: If you're clever, you don't have to find the exact milligram weight of each penny. Record in your lab notebook the date and any weight data you have for each penny.

Please do not break up the set. Return the entire set to your teacher when you finish.

_____

_____

_____

_____

a. In the year the penny's composition was changed, some of the pennies were made of copper and some of zinc. In what year was the change made? How do you know? On what property do you base your answer?

_____

_____

b. Calculate the average weight of a copper penny and the average weight of a zinc penny. (density Zn = 7.14 g/cm^3; density Cu = 8.92 g/cm^3.) How are these densities consistent with the relative weights of the two kinds of pennies?

_____

_____

c. Using the average weights of the zinc and copper pennies and the percentage of copper and zinc in each kind of penny, calculate the actual worth of each kind of penny in terms of zinc and copper prices. You'll need to get the current cost per pound of copper and of zinc from your teacher. A copper penny is 95% copper and 5% zinc:

$$\text{wt. (mg)} \times \frac{95 \text{ mg Cu}}{100 \text{ mg penny}} \times \frac{1 \text{ g Cu}}{1000 \text{ mg Cu}} \times \frac{1 \text{ pound Cu}}{454 \text{ g Cu}} \times \frac{\text{cost(\$) Cu}}{\text{pound of Cu}} = \$ \text{ Cu}$$

$$\text{wt. (mg)} \times \frac{5 \text{ mg Zn}}{100 \text{ mg penny}} \times \frac{1 \text{ g Zn}}{1000 \text{ mg Zn}} \times \frac{1 \text{ pound Zn}}{454 \text{ g Zn}} \times \frac{\text{cost (\$) Zn}}{\text{pound of Zn}} = \$ \text{ Zn}$$

A zinc penny is 2.4% copper and 97.6% zinc:

$$\text{wt. (mg)} \times \frac{2.4 \text{ mg Cu}}{100 \text{ mg penny}} \times \frac{1 \text{ g Cu}}{1000 \text{ mg Cu}} \times \frac{1 \text{ pound Cu}}{454 \text{ g Cu}} \times \frac{\text{cost (\$) Cu}}{\text{pound of Cu}} = \$ \text{ Cu}$$

$$\text{wt. (mg)} \times \frac{97.6 \text{ mg Zn}}{100 \text{ mg penny}} \times \frac{1 \text{ g Zn}}{1000 \text{ mg Zn}} \times \frac{1 \text{ pound Zn}}{454 \text{ g Zn}} \times \frac{\text{cost (\$) Zn}}{\text{pound of Zn}} = \$ \text{ Zn}$$

d. Any coin that is composed of metals worth less than the face value of the coin is called a subsidiary coin. Which of the two kinds of pennies is a subsidiary coin?

_____

_____

2. Devise a way to weigh a Sunday edition of a major newspaper by using your balance. Weigh the Sunday edition.

_____

5 ISOTOPES AND ATOMIC MASS

Small-Scale Experiment for text section 5.3

OBJECTIVES

- **Determine** the average weights of each isotope of the fictitious element vegium.
- **Determine** the relative abundance of isotopes of vegium.
- **Calculate** from experimental data the atomic mass of vegium.

INTRODUCTION

Isotopes are atoms of the same atomic number having different masses due to different numbers of neutrons. The atomic mass of an element is the weighted average of the masses of the isotopes of that element. The weighted average takes into account both the mass and relative abundance of each isotope as it occurs in nature. The relative abundances and masses of small atomic particles are measured in the laboratory by an instrument called a mass spectrometer. The mass spectrometer separates particles by mass and measures the mass and relative abundance of each. From these data a weighted average is calculated to determine the atomic mass of the element.

PURPOSE

In this lab you will carry out experiments and perform the necessary calculations to determine the atomic mass of the fictitious element vegium. The three different isotopes of vegium are beanium, peaium and cornium. As in real elements, these isotopes are collections of particles having different masses. Your job will be to obtain a sample of vegium and determine the relative abundance of each isotope and the mass of each type of particle. From this data you will calculate the weighted average mass, or atomic mass, of vegium. Unlike real isotopes, the individual isotopic particles of vegium differ slightly in mass, so you will determine the average mass of each type of isotopic particle. Then you can calculate the weighted average mass, or "atomic mass," of vegium.

SAFETY

- Behave in way that is consistent with a safe laboratory environment.

EQUIPMENT

a sample of vegium in a plastic cup
balance

EXPERIMENTAL PROCEDURE

Carry out the following steps, and record your results in Table 5.1.

1. Weigh all the beans, all the peas, and all the corn.

2. Count all the beans, all the peas, and all the corn.

3. Divide the mass of each isotope (beans, peas, and corn) by the number of each isotope to get the average mass of each isotope.

4. Divide the number of each isotope, the total number of particles, and multiply by 100 to get the percent abundance of each isotope.

5. Divide the percent abundance from Step 4 by 100 to get the relative abundance of each isotope.

6. Multiply the relative abundance from Step 5 by the average mass of each isotope to get the relative weight of each isotope.

7. Add the relative weights to get the average mass of all particles in vegium, the "atomic mass." Note: When you weigh the various isotopes of vegium, you may encounter some problems. For example, the sample of beans might be too large to weigh on your small-scale balance. You might solve this problem by making more weights or by using a larger counterweight on your small-scale balance. This approach increases the capacity of your small-scale balance. Keep in mind that it also results in a heavier beam, which reduces the sensitivity of your small-scale balance. Alternatively, you might weigh a portion of your vegetables, say half, and then multiply your result by two (or a fifth and multiply by five). The beans are of various sizes, so if you weigh just one bean and multiply by the number of beans to get the total weight of beans, a significant error might result. Weigh a large enough sample so you get a good estimation of the average weight of a bean.

Name _____ Class _____ Date _____

EXPERIMENTAL DATA

Record your results in Table 5.1 or a table like it in your notebook.

Table 5.1   "Atomic Mass" of Vegium

	Beans	Peas	Corn	Total
1. Mass of each isotope				
2. Number of each isotope				
3. Average mass of each				
4. Percent of each				
5. Relative Abundance				
6. Relative Weight				

CLEANING UP

Place the entire sample of vegium back in the plastic cup. Make sure that none of the particles are in the sink or on the floor.

QUESTIONS FOR ANALYSIS

Use what you learned in this lab to answer the following questions.

1. Which of your data in Table 5.1 must be measured and which can be calculated?

_____

_____

2. In all except Step 3 in Table 5.1, the numbers in the "Total" column can be obtained by adding the numbers across each row. Step 3 is an exception because it does not take into account the fact that there are different numbers of each kind of particle. Rather than add across, calculate this number in the same way you calculated the other numbers in row 3.

_____

3. What is the difference between percent and relative abundance?

_____

4. What is the result when you total the individual percentages? The individual relative abundances?

_____

5. The percentage of each vegetable tells you how many of each kind of vegetable there are in every 100 particles. What does relative abundance tell you?

_____

6. Compare the total values for Steps 3 and 6 on Table 5.1.

_____

7. Why can't atomic masses be calculated the way the total for row 3 is calculated?

_____

_____

_____

8. Explain any differences between the atomic mass of your vegium sample and that of your neighbor. Explain why the difference would be smaller if larger samples were used.

_____

_____

_____

NOW IT'S YOUR TURN!

1. Do the experiments to determine the atomic weight of a second sample of vegium. How does it compare to the first? Why?

_____

2. Select three beans from your sample—the largest, the smallest, and one bean that appears to be average in size. Determine the mass of each of the three. Compute the average mass of the largest and smallest, and compare this average to the mass of the "average" bean and to the average mass of beans you determined in Step 2 on Table 5.1. Which average mass do you think is most reliable? Why?

_____

_____

6 CHEMICAL NAMES AND FORMULAS

Small-Scale Experiment for text section 6.2

OBJECTIVES

- **Write** the chemical names and formulas of common chemical compounds.
- **Describe** the colors and textures of common ionic compounds.
- **Synthesize** chemical compounds, and write their names and formulas.

INTRODUCTION

Chemical substances are described not only by unique names but also by chemical formulas. A chemical name will describe a unique chemical formula and a chemical formula will have a unique chemical name. We use this language to communicate about chemistry.

All ions, of which some substances are made, have unique chemical names. The names and formulas of common monatomic and polyatomic anions and cations are listed below.

Name	Formula	Name	Formula
fluoride	F^-	oxide	O^{2-}
chloride	Cl^-	sulfide	S^{2-}
bromide	Br^-	sulfate	SO_4^{2-}
iodide	I^-	carbonate	CO_3^{2-}
acetate	CH_3COO^-	hydrogen phosphate	HPO_4^{2-}
nitrate	NO_3	phosphate	PO_4^{3-}
nitrite	NO_2^-		
hydroxide	OH^-		
hydrogen carbonate	HCO_3^-		
dihydrogen phosphate	$H_2PO_4^-$		

Name	Formula	Name	Formula
sodium	Na^+	magnesium	Mg^{2+}
potassium	K^+	calcium	Ca^{2+}
copper(I)	Cu^+	copper(II)	Cu^{2+}
ammonium	NH_4^+	iron(II)	Fe^{2+}
		iron(III)	Fe^{3+}
		lead(II)	Pb^{2+}
		lead(IV)	Pb^{4+}
		tin(II)	Sn^{2+}
		tin(IV)	Sn^{4+}

Most transition metals and the representative elements tin and lead form two or more cations. To distinguish different cations of the same element, a Roman numeral is used in the name to indicate the numerical value of the charge.

Cations and anions combine in a ratio that makes all ionic compounds electrically neutral. Formulas for ionic compounds are written so that the positive charge contributed by the cations exactly balances the negative charge contributed by the anions. For example, the formula for the ionic compound formed from Na^+ cations and O^{2-} anions is Na_2O. The formula for the cation is always written first. The subscript, 2, refers to two Na^+ ions that exactly balance the 2^- charge on one O^{2-} ion. To name an ionic compound, state the name of the cation and the name of the anion. Don't forget to use a Roman numeral to specify the numerical value of the positive charge of those atoms that form more than one cation. Some examples of formulas and names of ionic compounds are listed below.

Na_2O	sodium oxide	$CaSO_4$	calcium sulfate
KF	potassium fluoride	NH_4Br	ammonium bromide
FeS	iron(II) sulfide	$Cu_3(PO_4)_2$	copper(II) phosphate
$FeCl_3$	iron(III) chloride	$Pb(OH)_2$	lead(II) hydroxide

PURPOSE

In this lab you will observe and describe the colors and textures of various ionic compounds. Either the names or formulas of these compounds will be given. If the name is given, you will write its formula, and if the formula is given, you will write its name.

SAFETY

- Wear your safety glasses.
- Use full small-scale pipets only for the carefully controlled delivery of liquids.

EQUIPMENT

empty pipet for stirring
small-scale reaction surface with dried solid ionic compounds

Name _____ Class _____ Date _____

EXPERIMENTAL PAGE

1. Observe the solid compounds below. Write the color and any other descriptive information. If the name is given, write the formula. If the formula is given, write the name. Record your results in Table 6.1.

potassium iodide	sodium chloride	magnesium sulfate	copper(II) sulfate

$NaHCO_3$	$AgNO_3$	$NaNO_2$	KF

sodium carbonate	lead(II) nitrate	sodium acetate	ammonium chloride

sodium phosphate	calcium hydroxide	tin(IV) chloride	potassium bromide

$CaCl_2$	$FeCl_3$	Na_2HPO_4	NaH_2PO_4

Place this side of the Experimental Page facedown. Use the other side under your small-scale reaction surface.

EXPERIMENTAL DATA

Record your results in Table 6.1 or a table like it in your notebook.

Table 6.1   Names and Formulas of Ionic Solids

potasium iodide	sodium chloride	magnesium sulfate	copper(II) sulfate

_____ _____ _____ _____

$NaHCO_3$	$AgNO_3$	$NaNO_2$	KF

_____ _____ _____ _____

sodium carbonate	lead(II) nitrate	sodium acetate	ammonium chloride

_____ _____ _____ _____

sodium phosphate	calcium hydroxide	tin(IV) chloride	potassium bromide

_____ _____ _____ _____

$CaCl_2$	$FeCl_3$	Na_2HPO_4	NaH_2PO_4

_____ _____ _____ _____

CLEANING UP

Avoid contamination by cleaning up in a way that protects you and your environment. When you have finished answering the questions, return the small-scale reaction surface with its solid ionic compounds in place to your instructor.

Name _____ Class _____ Date _____

QUESTIONS FOR ANALYSIS

Use what you have learned in this lab to answer the following questions.

1. Write the formulas (with charges) and names of all the cations represented in this experiment.

   _____

   _____

2. Write the formulas (with charges) and names of all the anions represented in this experiment.

   _____

   _____

   _____

   _____

3. Write some simple rules for naming an ionic compound.

   _____

4. When is it appropriate to use Roman numerals in naming compounds?

   _____

5. What does a numerical subscript following an element in a chemical formula mean?

   _____

6. What does a numerical subscript following a set of parentheses in a chemical formula mean?

   _____

7. Write some simple rules for writing the formula for an ionic compound.

   _____

   _____

   _____

   _____

NOW IT'S YOUR TURN! 🥽

1. **a.** Place 1 drop of each solution in the indicated spaces below. Stir by blowing air from a dry pipet.

   b. Combine the ions to write the formulas of the chemical compounds that are produced by the mixings. Name each compound.

   c. What happened with each mixing? Make a table describing your results. Write the formula and name of each compound produced by the mixings.

	☠ $AgNO_3$ Ag^+	$Pb(NO_3)_2$ Pb^{2+} ☠			
$FeCl_3$ (Cl^-)	X	X			
KI (I^-)	X	X			
			$CuSO_4$ Cu^{2+}	$MgSO_4$ Mg^{2+}	$FeCl_3$ Fe^{3+}
$NaOH$ (OH^-) ☠	X	X	X	X	X
Na_2CO_3 (CO_3^{2-})	X	X	X	X	X
Na_3PO_4 (PO_4^{3-})	X	X	X	X	X

7 WEIGHING: A MEANS OF COUNTING

Small-Scale Experiment for text section 7.2

OBJECTIVES

- **Measure** masses of common compounds, objects, and minerals.
- **Calculate** moles and atoms from experimental masses.

INTRODUCTION

You can often measure how much of something you have by counting individual objects. For example, you can count the number of pennies you have in your pocket or the number of pencils you have in your locker. You learned in Chapter 7 that in chemistry there is a name for a number of atoms, ions, or molecules. One mole of a substance is equal to 6.02×10^{23} atoms, ions, or molecules of that substance. You also learned that you can "count" the number of moles in a substance by weighing the substance.

PURPOSE

In this lab you will measure the masses of samples of various common compounds like water, salt, and sugar. You will use your results as a means of counting the atoms, ions, and molecules in your samples. You will extend your technique to common objects that you can consider to be pure substances, like glass marbles, pieces of chalk, and polystyrene peanuts. Finally, you will measure the masses of various mineral samples and use your results to find the number of atoms in each.

SAFETY

- Behave in a way that is consistent with a safe laboratory.

MATERIALS

Solids: Sucrose ($C_{12}H_{22}O_{11}$), sodium chloride (NaCl), chalk ($CaCO_3$), glass slides, polystyrene peanuts, sulfur, fluorite, hematite, or other common minerals specified by your teacher.

EQUIPMENT

balance   plastic spoons

Name _____ Class _____ Date _____

EXPERIMENTAL PROCEDURE

1. Weigh one level teaspoon of sodium chloride, NaCl. Record its mass in Table 7.1. Repeat for one level teaspoon of water and one of sucrose, $C_{12}H_{22}O_{11}$.

2. Weigh a glass slide, and record its mass in Table 7.2. Repeat for a piece of chalk and a polystyrene peanut.

3. Weigh a piece of sulfur, and record its mass in Table 7.3. Repeat for a piece of fluorite and a piece of hematite.

EXPERIMENTAL DATA

Record your results in Tables 7.1, 7.2, and 7.3 or tables like them in your notebook.

Table 7.1 Counting Particles in Common Substances

	Name	Mass in mg	Molar mass	Moles in 1 teaspoon	Moles of each element	Atoms of each element
Formula NaCl	sodium chloride					
H_2O	water					
$C_{12}H_{22}O_{11}$	sucrose					

Table 7.2 Counting Particles in Common Items

	Name	Mass in mg	Molar mass	Moles in 1 sample	Moles of each element	Atoms of each element
Formula SiO_2	glass slide					
$CaCO_3$	chalk					
$(-CHCH_2-)_n$ | C_6H_5	polystyrene peanut					

Table 7.3 Counting Particles in Minerals

Formula	Mineral Name	Mass in mg	Molar mass	Moles	Moles of each element	Atoms of each element
S	sulfur					
CaF_2	fluorite					
Fe_2O_3	hematite					

CLEANING UP

Avoid contamination by cleaning up in a way that protects you and your environment. Return all the materials to their proper places. Sweep up and dispose of any spilled salt or sugar. Wash your hands thoroughly with soap and water.

QUESTIONS FOR ANALYSIS

Use what you learned in this lab to answer the following questions.

1. Calculate the number of moles of one level teaspoon of NaCl. Repeat for all the other compounds in Tables 7.1, 7.2, and 7.3.

$$x \text{ mol NaCl} = \text{wt. in mg NaCl} = \frac{1 \text{ g}}{1000 \text{ mg}} \times \frac{1 \text{ mol}}{58.5 \text{ g}} = \text{mol NaCl}.$$

2. Calculate the moles of each element in H_2O. Repeat for all the other compounds in Tables 7.1, 7.2, and 7.3.

$$x \text{ mol H} = \text{mol HOH} \times \frac{2 \text{ mol H}}{1 \text{ mol HOH}} = \text{mol H}$$

$$x \text{ mol O} = \text{mol HOH} \times \frac{1 \text{ mol O}}{1 \text{ mol HOH}} = \text{mol O}$$

3. Calculate the atoms of each element in H_2O. Repeat for all the other compounds in Tables 7.1, 7.2, and 7.3.

$$x \text{ atoms H} = \text{mol H} \times \frac{6.02 \times 10^{23} \text{ atoms}}{1 \text{ mol H}} = \text{atoms H}$$

4. In Step 1, you measured equal volumes of three different compounds. Which of the three compounds has the greatest number of moles in one teaspoon?

_____

5. Which of the three compounds in Step 1 has the greatest total number of atoms?

_____

Name _____ Class _____ Date _____

6. Why can we use the technique of measuring volume as a means of counting?

_____

_____

NOW IT'S YOUR TURN!

1. Design and carry out an experiment that will determine the number of atoms of calcium, carbon, and oxygen it takes to write your name on the chalkboard with a piece of chalk. Assume chalk is 100 percent calcium carbonate, $CaCO_3$.

_____

_____

2. A nickel coin is a mixture of metals called an alloy. It consists of 75 percent copper and 25 percent nickel. Design and carry out an experiment to find out how many nickel atoms there are in one 5-cent piece.

_____

$$x \text{ atoms} = \text{grams of coin} \times \frac{25 \text{ g Ni}}{100 \text{ g coin}} \times \frac{1 \text{ mol Ni}}{58.7 \text{ g}} \times \frac{6.02 \times 10^{23} \text{ atoms}}{\text{mol}}$$

3. A common mineral used in wallboard and plaster of Paris is gypsum, $CaSO_4 \cdot 2 H_2O$. Gypsum is an example of a hydrate. A hydrate is a compound that has water molecules incorporated into its crystal structure. The chemical formula of gypsum indicates that there are two water molecules for every calcium and sulfate ion within the crystal structure of gypsum. These water molecules are called water of hydration. Design an experiment to determine the number of water molecules in a sample of gypsum.

_____

$$x \text{ water molecules} = \text{grams gypsum} \times \frac{1 \text{ mol}}{172 \text{ g}} \times \frac{2 \text{ mol } H_2O}{1 \text{ mol gypsum}} \times \frac{6.02 \times 10^{23} \text{ molecules}}{1 \text{ mol}}$$

4. Determine the number of atoms in various samples of other minerals like graphite, C; barite, $BaSO_4$; Calcite, $CaCO_3$; pyrite, FeS_2; and galena, PbS_2.

_____

8 CHEMICAL EQUATIONS

For your course planning, you may not want to use this lab until Chapter 20.

OBJECTIVES

- **Classify** solutions as acids and bases.
- **Describe** chemical phenomena by writing chemical equations.
- **Identify** household products as acidic, basic, or neutral, on the basis of their reactions with indicators.
- **Investigate** the behavior of other synthetic and natural indicators in the presence of acids and bases.

INTRODUCTION

All chemical reactions involve changes in substances. These changes are often visible, and you call them macroscopic changes. Macroscopic changes can help you to classify chemical reactions. For example, in Small-Scale Experiment 1, the macroscopic changes you observed included the formation of precipitates, color changes, and the production of bubbles. The chemical reactions in Small-Scale Experiment 1 may be classified based on the macroscopic changes you observed.

To understand chemistry you must make many careful macroscopic observations and learn to infer from them the submicroscopic interactions of atoms and molecules. When chemical reactions occur, changes take place in individual atoms and molecules that cause the macroscopic changes you observe. A fundamental activity of chemistry is to try to find out what happens at the submicroscopic level.

To help you connect macroscopic changes and submicroscopic changes, chemical equations are used to represent symbolically what happens to atoms, ions, and molecules in chemical reactions. You learned in Section 8.1 that a chemical equation consists of an arrow separating the chemical formulas of the reactants (on the left) and the chemical formulas of products (on the right).

$$\text{reactants} \rightarrow \text{products}$$

Acids and bases are classified on the basis of their chemical properties. (Acids and bases are discussed more fully in Chapter 20.) Acids are recognized as a group of chemical compounds that have similar macroscopic chemical properties. They were originally classified on the basis of their sour taste (the word *acid* is derived from the Latin word for *sour*.) Further work showed that acids had other common properties, among them the ability to cause vegetable dyes to change colors and the ability to dissolve a wide variety of substances. Bases have a bitter taste and the ability to destroy or *neutralize* the properties of acids.

The fact that different acids show similar characteristic macroscopic chemical properties suggests that they are somehow related on the submicroscopic level. Similarly, bases must be related to each other.

The macroscopic changes associated with acids and bases are seen in changes in indicators. An indicator signals the occurrence of a chemical reaction by changing colors. You have already used phenolphthalein, a common synthetic acid-base indicator. Recall that it turned from colorless to bright pink in the presence of sodium hydroxide, a base. Other indicators exhibit other distinct color changes, signaling the occurrence of a chemical reaction.

PURPOSE

In this lab you will mix various solutions of acids and bases with an indicator and observe the macroscopic color changes that occur. You will classify solutions as acids or bases based on the color change they impart to the indicator, bromthymol blue, BTB. That is, you will classify solutions according to their macroscopic behavior. (Acids turn BTB yellow, and bases turn BTB blue.) Then you will repeat the experiment twice with two different indicators—phenolphthalein, phen, and bromphenol blue, BPB.

Finally, you will interpret your results in terms of submicroscopic properties, the behavior of atoms and molecules. You will learn how to express these unseen submicroscopic properties in a symbolic language of chemical formulas and equations. For example, one common submicroscopic property of acids is that they produce H_3O^+ ions in water. This can be explained by the following chemical equation:

$$HCl + H_2O \rightarrow H_3O^+ + Cl^-$$

The acid, HCl, transfers an H^+ ion to the water molecule to form H_3O^+.

SAFETY

- Wear your safety glasses.
- Use full small-scale pipets only for the carefully controlled delivery of liquids.

MATERIALS

Small-scale pipets of the following solutions:

sodium hydrogen carbonate ($NaHCO_3$)	ethanoic acid (CH_3COOH)
phosphoric acid (H_3PO_4)	sodium dihydrogen phosphate (NaH_2PO_4)
sodium hydroxide (NaOH)	nitric acid (HNO_3)
hydrochloric acid (HCl)	sodium carbonate (Na_2CO_3)
sodium hydrogen phosphate (Na_2HPO_4)	sodium phosphate (Na_3PO_4)
sodium hydrogen sulfate ($NaHSO_4$)	ammonia (NH_3)
sulfuric acid (H_2SO_4)	bromthymol blue (BTB)
sodium hydrogen sulfite ($NaHSO_3$)	phenolphthalein (phen)
bromphenol blue (BPB)	sodium ethanoate (CH_3COONa)

EQUIPMENT

empty pipet for stirring
small-scale reaction surface

Name _____ Class _____ Date _____

EXPERIMENTAL DATA

Record your results in Table 8.1 or a table like it in your notebook.

Table 8.1   Macroscopic and Submicroscopic Changes

a. BTB $NaHCO_3$ phen BPB		**f.** CH_3COONa		**k.** H_3PO_4	
b. BTB CH_3COOH phen BPB		**g.** NaOH		**l.** NaH_2PO_4	
c. BTB HCl phen BPB		**h.** HNO_3		**m.** Na_2HPO_4	
d. BTB Na_2CO_3 phen BPB		**i.** $NaHSO_4$		**n.** Na_3PO_4	
e. BTB H_2SO_4 phen BPB		**j.** NH_3		**o.** $NaHSO_3$	

CLEANING UP

Avoid contamination by cleaning up in a way that protects you and your environment. Carefully clean the reaction surface by absorbing the contents onto a paper towel, rinse the reaction surface with a damp paper towel, and dry it. Dispose of the paper towels in the waste bin.

QUESTIONS FOR ANALYSIS

Use what you learned in this lab to answer the following questions.

1. Define an acid and a base in terms of the color each turns BTB.

   _____

2. Name each acid and base you classified in this experiment. (See text Sections 6.4 and 6.5.)

   _____ _____ _____

   _____ _____ _____

   _____ _____ _____

   _____ _____ _____

   _____ _____ _____

Name _____ Class _____ Date _____

3. What is the common feature of the formula of each acid?

_____

4. What is an indicator? What purpose does it serve in this lab?

_____

_____

5. On a macroscopic level, your observations are that all acids turn BTB yellow. The common explanation on the submicroscopic level is that an acid produces H_3O^+ ions in water solution. Such submicroscopic interactions are described by the following symbolic representations, called chemical equations:

b. $CH_3COOH + H_2O \rightarrow H_3O^+ + CH_3COO^-$

c. $HCl + H_2O \rightarrow H_3O^+ + Cl^-$

i. $HSO_4^- + H_2O \rightarrow H_3O^+ + SO_4^{2-}$

Notice that in all three examples, a hydrogen ion, H^+, moves from the acid to a water molecule. Notice also that in **i**, you can take away the Na^+ ion before you write the equation. Write hydrogen-ion-transfer chemical equations, like the examples above, that describe the reactions of the other acids with water. Remember that whenever BTB turns yellow, one product is always H_3O^+.

_____

_____

_____

_____

_____

6. On a macroscopic level, a base turns BTB blue. The common explanation on the submicroscopic level is that a base produces OH^- ions in aqueous solution. Chemical equations to describe these interactions can be written like the ones below.

a. $HCO_3^- + HOH \rightarrow H_2CO_3 + OH^-$

j. $NH_3 + HOH \rightarrow NH_4^+ + OH^-$

Notice that in each case a base accepts a hydrogen ion, H^+, from a water molecule that forms a hydroxide ion, OH^-. Write hydrogen-ion-transfer chemical equations like the ones above to describe the reactions of the other bases with water. Every time you see BTB turn blue, one product is OH^-.

_____

_____

_____

_____

_____

7. Define an acid and a base in terms of what ions they produce in solution.

_____

8. What macroscopic changes did you find when you used phen and BPB to classify solutions as acids and bases?

_____

_____

NOW IT'S YOUR TURN!

1. Use BTB to classify several household products as acids or bases. Read the product labels to determine as best you can (name or formula) which acids or bases they contain. Organize your data into a concise table. While you're at it, test water from the tap.

2. BTB, BPB, and phen are only a few of many synthetic acid-base indicators. Design some experiments that use other indicators to classify the solutions you used in this lab as acids or bases. Tell what you did and make a table of your results. You may use any of the following synthetic indicators or any that your instructor provides:

methyl red, MR   alizarin yellow R, AYR
bromcresol green, BCG   thymol blue, TB
phenol red, PR   meta cresol purple, MCP

Hint: One such experiment might use methyl red, MR, to test both NaOH and HCl. You can then report the color of the indicator in each solution, draw a conclusion about the color the indicator changes in acid and base, and test your hypothesis by using other acids and bases. Finally, you can organize your results into a concise table. Cite advantages and disadvantages of using other indicators to classify acids and bases.

3. Many common substances also act as acid-base indicators. Design and carry out an experiment to use some or all of these to classify solutions as acids or bases. Tell what you do and make a table of your results. Try several of the following: grape juice, cabbage juice, food dyes, flower petals, vegetable juices, fabric dyes, and water-soluble pen inks. Can you think of anything else to try?

BALANCING CHEMICAL EQUATIONS

Small-Scale Experiment for text section 8.2

OBJECTIVES

- **Probe** the occurrence of neutralization reactions by using an acid–base indicator.
- **Balance** chemical equations that describe reactions between acids and bases.
- **Test** other means to detect neutralization reactions.

INTRODUCTION

In Small-Scale Experiment 8 you saw that acids and bases can be distinguished by the color changes they induce in indicators. For example, bromthymol blue is yellow in acid solution and blue in basic solution.

On the submicroscopic level, acids produce H_3O^+ ions in solution, and bases produce OH^- ions in solution. Acids and bases also react with each other in what is called a *neutralization reaction*. In general, an acid and a hydroxide base react to produce a salt and water. A salt is any ionic compound produced by a neutralization reaction. For example, the reaction of hydrochloric acid, HCl, with sodium hydroxide, NaOH, produces sodium chloride, NaCl, and water. The chemical equation that represents this neutralization reaction is written as follows:

$$HCl + NaOH \rightarrow NaCl + HOH$$

$$acid + base \rightarrow salt + water$$

Two more examples of neutralization reactions follow here:

$$H_2SO_4 + 2NaOH \rightarrow Na_2SO_4 + 2HOH$$

$$acid + base \rightarrow salt + water$$

$$H_3PO_4 + 3KOH \rightarrow K_3PO_4 + 3HOH$$

$$acid + base \rightarrow salt + water$$

Notice that each equation is balanced; there are the same number of each kind of atom on both sides of the equation. Notice also that these neutralization reactions are examples of double-replacement reactions (Section 8.2), which involve an exchange of positive ions between two compounds. In the examples above, a potassium or sodium ion is exchanged with a hydrogen ion.

PURPOSE

In this lab you will use bromthymol blue, as well as other probes, to examine neutralization reactions more closely and learn to balance the chemical equations that describe them. An indicator is usually necessary to detect acid–base neutralization reactions because often the reaction is invisible without an indicator. The reason is that often both the reactants and the products of neutralization reactions are colorless solutions. You can use an acid–base indicator such as BTB to detect a neutralization reaction.

SAFETY

- Wear your safety glasses.
- Use full small-scale pipets only for the carefully controlled delivery of liquids.

MATERIALS

Small-scale pipets of the following solutions:
calcium hydroxide (Ca(OH)$_2$)
ammonia (NH$_3$)
bromthymol blue (BTB)

phosphoric acid (H$_3$PO$_4$)
hydrochloric acid (HCl)
nitric acid (HNO$_3$)
sulfuric acid (H$_2$SO$_4$)
ethanoic acid (CH$_3$COOH)

sodium hydroxide (NaOH)
potassium hydroxide (KOH)

EQUIPMENT

small-scale reaction surface
glass slide
cotton swab
hot plate
empty pipet for stirring

Name _____ Class _____ Date _____

EXPERIMENTAL DATA

1. Record your results in Table 9.1 or a table like it in your notebook.

Table 9.1   Reactions of Acids and Bases

Bases	Strong Acids			Weak Acids	
	HCl	HNO$_3$	H$_2$SO$_4$	CH$_3$COOH	H$_3$PO$_4$
NaOH					
KOH					
Ca(OH)$_2$					
NH$_3$ (NH$_4$OH)					

2. What did you observe when you mixed an acid and base without BTB as an indicator? Why is the indicator necessary to detect these reactions?

_____

3. What happened when you added a few drops of base to each yellow mixture?

_____

4. What did you observe when you evaporated the mixtures on a hot plate?

_____

5. What happened to the ammonia odor from the cotton swab when you added HCl?

_____

CLEANING UP

Avoid contamination by cleaning up in a way that protects you, your neighbors, and your environment. Carefully clean the small-scale reaction surface by absorbing the contents onto a paper towel (not onto your hands). Rinse the reaction surface with a damp paper towel and dry it. Dispose of the paper towels in the waste bin. Clean the glass slide, rinse it thoroughly with water, and dry it with a paper towel. Wash your hands thoroughly with soap and water.

Name _____ Class _____ Date _____

QUESTIONS FOR ANALYSIS

Use what you learned in this lab to answer the following questions.

1. Why is the indicator necessary to detect these reactions?

   _____

2. Besides indicators, what other ways are there to detect neutralization?

   _____

3. What is the chemical formula for ethanoic acid? What is its common name?

   _____

4. The complete chemical equations for reactions **a–e** on the Experimental Page are listed below. Balance each equation by placing the proper coefficient in front of each chemical formula so that each side of the equation has the same number of atoms of each element.

   a. ____ $NaOH$ + ____ $HCl \rightarrow$ ____ $NaCl$ + ____ HOH

   b. ____ $NaOH$ + ____ $HNO_3 \rightarrow$ ____ $NaNO_3$ + ____ HOH

   c. ____ $NaOH$ + ____ $H_2SO_4 \rightarrow$ ____ Na_2SO_4 + ____ HOH

   d. ____ $NaOH$ + ____ $CH_3COOH \rightarrow$ ____ CH_3COONa + ____ HOH

   e. ____ $NaOH$ + ____ $H_3PO_4 \rightarrow$ ____ Na_3PO_4 + ____ HOH

5. Write down the chemical formulas for the reactants for reactions **f–j** on the Experimental Page. Now write an arrow and the formulas of the products. Finally, balance each chemical equation you write. (Hint: Equations **f–j** will look just like equations **a–e**, except K replaces Na.)

   _____

   _____

   _____

   _____

   _____

6. Balance equations **k–o**, below.

   k. ____ $Ca(OH)_2$ + ____ $HCl \rightarrow$ ____ $CaCl_2$ + ____ HOH

   l. ____ $Ca(OH)_2$ + ____ $HNO_3 \rightarrow$ ____ $Ca(NO_3)_2$ + ____ HOH

   m. ____ $Ca(OH)_2$ + ____ $H_2SO_4 \rightarrow$ ____ $CaSO_4$ + ____ HOH

   n. ____ $Ca(OH)_2$ + ____ $CH_3COOH \rightarrow$ ____ $(CH_3COO)_2Ca$ + ____ HOH

   o. ____ $Ca(OH)_2$ + ____ $H_3PO_4 \rightarrow$ ____ $Ca_3(PO_4)_2$ + ____ HOH

7. Ammonia is a base and reacts with water to produce ammonium ion and hydroxide ion:

$$NH_3 + HOH \rightarrow NH_4^+ + OH^-$$

Often the formula for aqueous ammonia is written as if it were ammonium hydroxide, NH_4OH. Balance equations **p–t** below.

p. ____ NH_4OH + ____ $HCl \rightarrow$ ____ NH_4Cl + ____ HOH

q. ____ NH_4OH + ____ $HNO_3 \rightarrow$ ____ NH_4NO_3 + ____ HOH

r. ____ NH_4OH + ____ $H_2SO_4 \rightarrow$ ____ $(NH_4)_2SO_4$ + ____ HOH

s. ____ NH_4OH + ____ $CH_3COOH \rightarrow$ ____ CH_3COONH_4 + ____ HOH

t. ____ NH_4OH + ____ $H_3PO_4 \rightarrow$ ____ $(NH_4)_3PO_4$ + ____ HOH

8. Define neutralization. Write a chemical equation to illustrate your answer.

_____

_____

9. Define a salt. Write the chemical formulas for examples from this experiment.

_____

_____

10. What is a double-replacement reaction? How is a double replacement reaction different from a single-replacement reaction?

_____

_____

11. Give two ways of expressing the formula for water. In this lab, did water act as an acid or a base? Explain.

_____

12. Upon evaporation of the NaOH + HCl reaction, what is the name and chemical formula of the white solid that remains? Write a chemical equation to explain your answer.

_____

13. What happened to the ammonia odor when you added HCl to it? Write a chemical equation to explain your answer.

_____

_____

Name _____ Class _____ Date _____

NOW IT'S YOUR TURN!

1. Design an experiment using several different indicators to detect neutralization reactions. Write down what you do, what happens, and what it means. Design a concise data table to summarize your results.

_____

_____

2. Design an experiment to see if you can neutralize the ammonia odor with acids other than hydrochloric acid.

_____

3. Describe a procedure you would use to neutralize the ammonia smell in household ammonia or glass cleaner. Try it in the lab! Can a similar procedure be used to neutralize the smell of vinegar, CH_3COOH? Try it in the lab! Does your procedure work to neutralize the smell of other acids like lemon juice?

_____

_____

_____

4. Antacids are so named because they are designed to neutralize stomach acid (HCl). Design some experiments using indicators to show that antacids really do neutralize acids. Use acids other than just HCl. Write down each experiment you do, what happens, and what it means.

_____

_____

TITRATION: DETERMINING HOW MUCH ACID IS IN A SOLUTION

Small-Scale Experiment for text section 9.2

OBJECTIVES

- **Demonstrate** an understanding of the meaning of each of the following terms: qualitative, quantitative, calibration, titration, equivalence point, end point.
- **Calibrate** pipets by measuring volumes of drops.
- **Measure** the molar concentration of acid solutions by using the technique of titration.

INTRODUCTION

If you read the label on a typical chemical consumer product, you can often find both qualitative and quantitative information. Qualitative information answers the question, "What?" Quantitative information answers the question, "How much?" For example, a typical bottle of toilet bowl cleaner tells you that it contains 9.5% (how much) hydrochloric acid, HCl (what). Hydrochloric acid is the "active ingredient," the ingredient that performs the specific function for which the product is designed. Hydrochloric acid helps dissolve mineral deposits that build up on the inside of the toilet bowl.

A *titration* is a way to measure the number of moles of a substance dissolved in a liter of solution. The resulting quantity is called the molarity of the substance and is expressed in units of moles per liter (mol/L) or simply *M*. An acid–base titration typically uses a known amount of base to measure an unknown amount of acid in a solution. In a typical titration, you slowly add a base with a known concentration, like NaOH, to a measured volume of unknown acid solution, such as HCl. The neutralization reaction occurs:

$$acid + base \rightarrow salt + water$$
$$HCl + NaOH \rightarrow NaCl + HOH$$

When all the acid is just neutralized by the base, the *equivalence point* has been reached. (The number of moles of base is equivalent to the number of moles of acid at the equivalence point.) You use the volume of base needed to reach the equivalence point to calculate how many moles of acid were neutralized by that volume of base. Because the reactants and products are colorless, it is often necessary to use an indicator to determine the equivalence point of the reaction. Phenolphthalein is an indicator that is colorless in acid solution but bright pink in basic solution. If phenolphthalein is present in the titration mixture, it will remain colorless until 1 drop of base neutralizes the last of the acid and makes the solution very slightly basic. At this point, called the *end point*, a dramatic color change from colorless to pink occurs.

Notice that the end point and the equivalence point are not necessarily the same. In the case of phenolphthalein, the end point occurs when the solution turns just slightly basic, not when the solution is exactly neutral, the equivalence point. Accurate titrations require the use of an indicator that will give an end point that is very close to the equivalence point.

PURPOSE

In this lab you will use the quantitative technique of titration to determine the concentrations in moles per liter, M, of various acid samples using exactly $0.50M$ sodium hydroxide, NaOH. In a typical experiment, you will deliver a specific number of drops of an acid to a reaction vessel and add an indicator like phenolphthalein. You will then count the number of drops of NaOH that is needed to turn the indicator pink. To find the volume of a drop, you will calibrate pipets by counting the number of drops each pipet delivers to fill the same size volume. You will carry out several experiments to determine what is the best way to calibrate (measure the drop size of) a pipet so that it always delivers the same size drops. Calibration is a way to correct for the different-sized drops delivered by different pipets.

SAFETY

- Wear your safety glasses.
- Use full small-scale pipets only for the carefully controlled delivery of liquids.

MATERIALS

Small-scale pipets of the following solutions:
ethanoic acid (CH₃COOH)   phenolphthalein (phen)

hydrochloric acid (HCl)
nitric acid (HNO₃)
sulfuric acid (H₂SO₄)

sodium hydroxide (NaOH)

EQUIPMENT

well plate
plastic cup
cotton swab

EXPERIMENTAL PROCEDURE

Part A. Calibrating a Small-Scale Pipet: Measuring the Relative Sizes of Drops

1. Perform a series of experiments that will answer the following questions. Work individually, as it is important that you become skilled in calibrations. Record your results in Table 11.1.

   a. How many drops of water from a small-scale pipet are needed to fill a well? Can you repeat this result?

   b. What is the best way to tell exactly when the well is full?

   c. Is it important to expel the air bubble before you begin?

   d. Try delivering drops with the pipet vertical, horizontal, and at a 45° angle. At which angle do you obtain the most number of drops? The least? Which angle delivers the smallest drops?

e. What will happen if you do not always hold the pipet at the same angle?

   f. Do different pipets give different results at the same angle? Why is it important to calibrate each different pipet you use?

2. Calibrate an HCl pipet and a NaOH pipet. Count the number of drops of each needed to fill a well for each substance. Repeat until your results are reproducible. Record your results in Table 10.2.

Part B. The Titration

3. Carry out a titration of HCl as follows:

   a. Holding the pipet vertically, count 20 drops of HCl into a plastic cup. Take care not to touch the ends of the pipet to the cup or to the solution in the cup. Let D_a equal this number of drops.

   b. Add one drop of phenolphthalein to the HCl in the cup.

   c. Add NaOH slowly, counting the number of drops of NaOH needed to obtain a stable pink end point. As you titrate, swirl the cup gently. Let D_b equal this number of drops.

   d. Repeat Steps **a–c** in a clean, dry cup until your results are consistent.

4. Titrate HNO_3 and CH_3COOH, each with NaOH in the same way. Here are some tips for accuracy and to avoid contamination. Use a clean cup. Take care not to let the ends of the pipets touch the cup or the solution in the cup. Hold the pipets vertically. As you titrate, swirl gently and count the number of drops of NaOH it takes to get a stable pink color. Clean and dry the cup before each titration. When the pipets are empty, take care to refill them with the proper solutions. Read the labels twice!

Name _____ Class _____ Date _____

EXPERIMENTAL DATA

Record the results of your calibrations and titrations in Tables 10.1, 10.2, and 10.3 or tables like them in your notebook.

Table 10.1   Calibration of Small-Scale Pipet

| | Drops to fill | | |
	Trial 1	Trial 2	Trial 3
Vertical			
Horizontal			
45° angle			

Summarize a method that will always accurately *calibrate* or determine the number of drops delivered by any pipet to fill a well.

_____

_____

Table 10.2   Calibration of HCl and NaOH Pipets

| | Drops to fill | | |
	Trial 1	Trial 2	Trial 3
HCl			
NaOH			

Table 10.3   Titrations of Acids

Acid		Drops to fill C_a	Drops NAOH to fill C_b	Drops NaOH to pink D_b	M of acid M_a
	HCl				
	HCl				
	HNO$_3$				
	HNO$_3$				
	CH$_3$COOH				
	CH$_3$COOH				

Calculate the molar concentration, M_a of HCl and of the other two acids by substituting the following pieces of data into the expression below.

M_b = molar concentration of NaOH (M_b = 0.50 M in this experiment)

D_a = drops of acid used (20 drops in this experiment)

D_b = drops of NaOH to pink end point

C_a = drops of acid needed to fill a well

C_b = drops of NaOH needed to fill a well

$$M_a = \frac{M_b \times D_b}{D_a} \times \frac{C_a}{C_b}$$

_____

_____

_____

CLEANING UP

Avoid contamination by cleaning up in a way that protects you and your environment. Carefully clean the plastic cup and well-strip by disposing of the liquid contents in the sink and rinsing them thoroughly with water. Dry both pieces of equipment with a paper towel. Wash your hands thoroughly with soap and water.

Name _____ Class _____ Date _____

QUESTIONS FOR ANALYSIS

Use what you learned in this lab to answer the following questions.

1. What is an acid–base titration? Is titration a qualitative or quantitative method? Explain.

   _____

   _____

2. What does it mean to calibrate a pipet? Is calibration a qualitative or quantitative method? Explain.

   _____

   _____

3. Why is it important to calibrate each pipet when measuring the volumes of solutions?

   _____

4. Why is it important to repeat a calibration or a titration until the results are consistent?

   _____

   _____

5. Summarize the steps it takes to calibrate a small-scale pipet.

   _____

   _____

6. Why do your calculations of acid concentrations include the number of drops of NaOH and HCl needed to fill a well?

   _____

   _____

7. Write the chemical equation for each titration reaction you carried out in this experiment.

   _____

   _____

   _____

8. Write the balanced equation for the reaction of sulfuric acid, H_2SO_4, with sodium hydroxide, NaOH. How is it different from the equations you wrote for the reactions of HCl, HNO_3, and CH_3COOH with NaOH?

   _____

   _____

9. Sulfuric acid, H_2SO_4, is an example of a "diprotic" acid. Explain what this means. Give an example of a "triprotic" acid. Give two examples of monoprotic acids.

_____

_____

NOW IT'S YOUR TURN!

1. Let's explore titration a little further. To carry out a "serial titration," add four drops of HCL + one drop phen to a 1×12 well plate as shown below.

1   2   3   4   5   6   7   8   9   10   11   12

Then add: 1   2   3   4   5   6   7   8   9   10   11   12   drops of NaOH.

(Add the number of drops of NaOH = to the well number.) Record your results.

a. Which wells have more acid than base? Which have more base than acid?

_____

b. The end point is the point at which the indicator changes colors. Which well represents the end point of the titration?

_____

c. The equivalence point is the point at which enough base is added to just neutralize the acid. (The moles of base are "equal" to the moles of acid.) Which well represents the "equivalence point?"

_____

d. How does the equivalence point differ from the end point? By how many drops, at most, is the equivalence point different from the end point?

_____

_____

e. What is the absolute error in this experiment?

_____

2. Design titration experiments to determine the molar concentration of H_2SO_4. Be sure to calibrate each pipet you use and run each experiment at least twice so you can be confident of your answers. If you calculate the molar concentration of H_2SO_4 in the same way as the other acids, your result will be off by a factor of two. Where does the factor of 2 go in the molarity calculation?

3. Some toilet bowl cleaners are water solutions containing hydrochloric acid, HCl. Vinegar is a water solution of ethanoic acid, CH_3COOH. Design experiments to determine the molar concentrations of HCl in various household products and of ethanoic acid, CH_3COOH, in vinegar. Be sure to calibrate the pipets you use. Organize your results into a table like Table 10.3 and report your calculations in your laboratory notebook. Note: Because some of the solutions are highly colored, the end point might not be pink. Try using 3 drops phen and look for the end point to be a distinct color change.

⓫ WEIGHT TITRATIONS: MEASURING MOLAR CONCENTRATIONS

Small-Scale Experiment for text section 9.2

OBJECTIVES

- **Measure** the molar concentration of acids using weight titrations.
- **Compare** the accuracy of weight titrations with that of volumetric titrations.
- **Identify** unknown solutions by applying both qualitative and quantitative analysis.

INTRODUCTION

A *weight titration* is a method of finding molar concentration by weighing solutions rather than measuring their volumes. A weight titration is often more accurate than a volumetric titration because a balance is usually a more accurate instrument than a pipet. The result of a weight titration depends only on weights determined directly from the balance and not on volumes determined from pipets.

You can use the balance to determine the volumes of solutions by weighing. You know that the density of water is one gram per cubic centimeter or one milligram per microliter. The densities of dilute aqueous solutions are assumed to be equal to the density of water. This means that if you weigh a solution in milligrams, it has the same numerical volume in microliters.

PURPOSE

In this lab you will carry out a weight titration. You will weigh a certain amount of acid solution and add an indicator. Then you will determine the weight of NaOH you need to add to reach the end point. To do this using a small-scale balance you will zero your balance with a pipet full of NaOH. There is no need to weigh the pipet as you only need to know the *difference* in weight before and after the titration. Next, you will add NaOH to the acid solution until the indicator changes. Finally, you will determine the weight of the NaOH needed for the titration by placing the pipet back on the small-scale balance and adding weights to make up for the NaOH we used. The total weight you add is the weight of the NaOH that was used in the titration.

Notice that you do not have to count drops. You do not have to hold the pipet at any particular angle. You do not have to be careful to expel any air bubbles.

SAFETY 👓

- Wear your safety glasses.
- Use full small-scale pipets only for the carefully controlled delivery of liquids.

MATERIALS

Small-scale pipets of the following solutions:
phenolphthalein (phen)   ethanoic acid (CH₃COOH)

sodium hydroxide (NaOH)

hydrochloric acid (HCl)
nitric acid (HNO₃)
sulfuric acid (H₂SO₄)

EQUIPMENT

balance
plastic cup

EXPERIMENTAL PROCEDURE

1. Weigh 500 mg of acid solution on your small-scale balance as follows:

    a. Place a 500 mg weight in a clean, dry cup.

    b. Set the balance so the pointer reads zero.

    c. Remove the weight and add acid until the pointer again reads zero.

2. Add 5 drops of phen.

3. Weigh or tare two full NaOH pipets. (If you tare the pipets there is no need to weigh them!)

    a. Place two pipets of NaOH in a second clean, dry cup.

    b. Set the balance so it reads zero. (Use two pipets just to make sure we have enough NaOH.)

4. Titrate the acid solution in the first cup with NaOH from one of the pipets until *1 drop* turns the solution to a stable pink color.

5. Determine the weight of the NaOH used for the titration. Record this weight in Table 11.1.

    a. Return both of the NaOH pipets to the second cup.

    b. Add weights until the balance pointer again reads zero. The sum of the added weights is the weight of the NaOH used in the titration.

6. Repeat Steps 1–5 until you obtain consistent results. (The only way to tell whether you result is reliable is to reproduce it!)

7. Design and carry out weight titrations to determine the molar concentrations of nitric acid, HNO₃; sulfuric acid, H₂SO₄; and ethanoic acid, CH₃COOH. Titrate each acid at least twice.

EXPERIMENTAL DATA

Record your results in Table 11.1 or a table like it in your notebook.

Table 11.1   Molarity of Acids

	HCl	HCl	HNO$_3$	HNO$_3$	H$_2$SO$_4$	H$_2$SO$_4$	CH$_3$COOH	CH$_3$COOH
Weight of acid (mg)								
Weight of NaOH (mg)								
Molarity of acid (M)								

Calculate the molar concentration of HCl in each sample. Record them in Table 11.1. Do the same calculation for the titrations of HNO$_3$, H$_2$SO$_4$, and CH$_3$COOH. Note: When calculating the molar concentration of H$_2$SO$_4$, you must divide your result by 2 because there are 2 moles of acidic hydrogens per mole of sulfuric acid.

$$\text{Molarity of acid} = \frac{(\text{molarity of NaOH})(\text{weight of NaOH in mg})}{(\text{weight of HCl in mg})}$$

In this experiment the molarity of NaOH is 0.5M.

CLEANING UP

Avoid contamination by cleaning up in a way that protects you and your environment. Carefully clean the plastic cup by disposing of the liquid contents, rinsing the cup thoroughly with water, and drying it with a paper towel. Dispose of the paper towels in the waste bin. Wash your hands thoroughly with soap and water.

QUESTIONS FOR ANALYSIS

Use what you learned in this lab to answer the following questions.

1. Why is it that when you weigh a dilute solution, the number of milligrams of solution is equal to the number of microliters of solution?

_____

_____

2. When using a small-scale balance, why is it not necessary to weigh the NaOH pipet before you begin titrating?

_____

_____

3. Why is it not important to expel the air bubble or hold the pipet at a vertical angle when you titrate?

_____

4. Explain how you can determine the weight of the NaOH used in the titration without ever knowing the weight of the pipet or its contents.

_____

_____

_____

_____

NOW IT'S YOUR TURN!

1. Your instructor will give you a list of consumer products to titrate. Use the Experimental Procedure in this lab to titrate each consumer product at least twice, or until you obtain consistent results. Substitute the HCl in this experiment for the consumer product containing HCl or another acid. Make a table in which to record your data, and report the name of the product, the weight of the product sample, the weight of the NaOH needed to titrate it, and the calculated molar concentration of HCl or other acid in the product.

a. Use your data for the titration of household products to calculate the % HCl in each household product, and record it in a table.

$$\% \text{ HCl} = \frac{g\ HCL}{100\ g\ soln} = \frac{no.\ mol\ HCL}{L\ soln} \times \frac{36.5\ g\ HCL}{mol\ HCl} \times \frac{1\ L\ soln}{1000\ g\ soln} \times 100$$

(The molecular weight of HCl is 36.5 g/mol. The density of each solution is taken to be 1000 g/L.)

b. Read each household product's label and find the % HCl listed. Compare each to your calculated values. Calculate the % error for each.

$$\% \text{ error} = \frac{|calculated\ value - product\ label\ value|}{product\ label\ value} \times 100$$

c. Are your values necessarily in error? Explain. What factors might account for the differences?

_____

d. Use your data for the titration of vinegar to calculate the % CH_3COOH in vinegar and record it in a table.

$$\% \text{ } CH_3OOH = \frac{g\ CH_3COOH}{100\ g\ soln} = \frac{no.\ mol\ CH_3\ COOH}{L\ soln} \times \frac{60\ g\ CH_3COOH}{mol\ CH_3\ COOH} \times \frac{1\ L\ soln}{1000\ g\ soln} \times 100$$

(The molecular weight of CH_3COOH is 60 g/mol. The density of each solution is taken to be 1000 g/L.)

e. Calculate the percent error of ethanoic acid, CH_3COOH, in vinegar.

2. Now you know how to determine the molar concentration of an acid. This is *quantitative analysis*. Quantitative analysis answers the question, "How much?" However, you also need to know what the acid is. *Qualitative analysis* answers the question, "What is it?"

a. Below is a design for an experiment to study and compare the reactions of various acids. You can use their differences to identify what they are.

Mix 1 drop of each of these compounds in the indicated space.

	BTB	UI	Na_2CO_3	$Pb(NO_3)_2$	$AgNO_3$	$CaCl_2$
HCl				X	X	X
HNO_3				X	X	X
H_2SO_4				X	X	X
CH_3COOH				X	X	X

Which reactions are the same for all the acids? Which reactions are different and therefore afford a way to distinguish the acids?

b. Obtain 3 *unknown acids* from your instructor. Design some experiments to identify the acids (qualitative analysis) and to determine their molar concentrations (quantitative analysis.) Report your results as instructed.

12 ABSORPTION OF WATER BY PAPER TOWELS: A CONSUMER LAB

Small-Scale Experiment for text section 10.2

OBJECTIVES

- **Measure** the amounts of water absorbed by various commercial paper towels.
- **Measure** the strengths of various brands of paper towels when wet.
- **Measure** the time it takes paper towels to absorb water.
- **Compare** the properties of various brands of paper towels.
- **Determine** the best brand for the money.

INTRODUCTION

Each paper-towel manufacturer goes to great lengths to persuade consumers that its brand is better than all the others. Eye-catching packaging and decorator designs compete for your attention on the supermarket shelves. At certain times of the year, you can even buy paper towels with holiday themes. Television commercials pitch the various virtues of paper towels: how much moisture they absorb, how fast they do it, and how strong they are when wet. Even microwaveability is touted.

Is one paper towel really better than another? Does price reflect quality? What does it mean to be better? Stronger? Faster? More absorbent?

PURPOSE

In this lab you will attempt to answer some of these questions and along the way you will formulate even more questions. You will begin by examining several properties of various brands of paper towels. You will weigh a dry paper towel, wet it, and weigh it again to see how much water it picked up. You will test its speed of absorbancy by measuring the time it takes to absorb a certain amount of water. Finally, you will test the wet strength of paper towels to determine how well they hold up to tough jobs. You will then compile your results and compare these results with the price of each product to try to determine the best buy in the paper-towel market.

SAFETY

- Behave in a way that is consistent with a safe laboratory.

EQUIPMENT

several brands of paper towels with their labels	1/4-inch office hole punch
a 5 cm × 10 cm card	plastic cup
scissors	clothespins
balance	water (H_2O)
	soda straws

EXPERIMENTAL PROCEDURE

Part A. How much water does each towel pick up?

1. Cut a 5 cm × 10 cm piece of paper towel. Use the card as a template to cut the paper towel to the right size. Weigh it dry. Record its weight in Table 12.1.

2. Fold the paper towel in half the long way and wet it thoroughly in a cup half full of water.

3. When removing the towel from the water, skim it across the lip of the cup to remove excess water. Weigh the towel wet. Record its weight in Table 12.1.

4. Repeat this procedure for several brands of paper towels.

Part B. How fast does each towel pick up water?

5. Make a straw stand on your balance base to hang paper towels as in Figure 12.1. Hang a 5 cm × 10 cm piece of paper towel from the stand by a clothespin so that 1 cm of the bottom is immersed in a cup of water. Measure the time it takes for the water to travel 2 centimeters. Repeat for the other brands of towels. Record your results in Table 12.2.

Figure 12.1 *Straw stand for paper towels*

Part C. How strong is each wet towel?

6. Attach 2 clothespins, one to each end of a 1 cm × 10 cm piece of paper towel, and wet the towel in the middle. Be sure the wet part does not touch either clothespin. Hold one clothespin in your hand and attach clothespins, one at a time, to the other clothespins. Count the number of clothespins that are needed to break the wet towel. Record your results in Table 12.3.

Part D. How do the paper towels compare in price?

7. Read the labels on each brand of paper towel you measured. Find the following data and record it in Table 12.4

   a. The price per roll.

   b. The number of square feet of paper per roll.

   c. The number of square feet you can buy for a penny.

   $$x = \frac{\text{square feet}}{\text{penny}} = \frac{\text{number of sq. ft}}{\text{roll}} \times \frac{1 \text{ roll}}{\text{price pennies}}$$

   d. Calculate the milligrams of water absorbed per penny.

   $$x = \frac{\text{mg}}{\text{penny}} = \frac{\text{square feet}}{\text{penny}} \times \frac{929 \text{ cm}^2}{\text{square foot}} \times \frac{\text{no. of mg absorbed}}{50 \text{ cm}^2}$$

Name _____ Class _____ Date _____

EXPERIMENTAL DATA

Record your results in Tables 12.1, 12.2, 12.3 and 12.4 or tables like them in your notebook.

Table 12.1   How much water does each towel pick up?

Brand of towel	A	B	C	D	E
Wet weight (mg)					
Dry weight (mg)					
Water weight (mg)					
Relative water weight					

What is the wet weight and dry weight of each brand of paper towel, and how many milligrams of water does each pick up? To find the "relative water weight," divide all the "water weights" by the lowest "water weight." This will tell you how many times better each towel is at picking up water compared to the worst one. Record your data in Table 12.1 or a table like it.

Table 12.2   How fast does each towel pick up water?

Brand of towel	A	B	C	D	E
Time to absorb 2 cm. (s)					

Table 12.3   How strong is each wet towel?

Brand of towel	A	B	C	D	E
Number of clothespins					

Name _____ Class _____ Date _____

Table 12.4   How do the paper towels compare in price?

Brand of towel	A	B	C	D	E
Price per roll ($)					
Square feet per roll					
Square feet per penny					
mg water absorbed per ¢					

CLEANING UP

Avoid contamination by cleaning up in a way that protects you and your environment. Please recycle all usable pieces of paper towels. Dispose of unusable scraps in the waste bin.

QUESTIONS FOR ANALYSIS

Use what you learned in this lab to answer the following questions.

1. Which paper towel is the most absorbent? The least?

_____

2. Which paper towel absorbed moisture faster than all the others? Slower than all the others?

_____

3. Which is the strongest paper towel? Which is the weakest?

_____

NOW IT'S YOUR TURN!

1. Why is it important to do the strength test in Step 6 with clothespins touching only dry parts of the towel? Repeat the experiment so the clothespins are touching the wet part.

_____

_____

2. What other paper can you try at home?

_____

13 HEAT OF FUSION OF ICE

Small-Scale Experiment for text section 11.3

OBJECTIVES

- **Measure** temperature changes when ice melts in water.
- **Calculate** heat changes from experimental data.
- **Calculate** the heat of fusion of ice from experimental data.

INTRODUCTION

Consider this. You pop the top on the can of your favorite soft drink and pour it over ice. Does the soft drink become cold simply because the ice is cold or is there more to it than that? You know that heat always flows from a warm object to a cooler one. For example, when you place your hand on a cold window, your hand gets cold. Heat flows from your hand to the window giving your hand a cooling sensation. Similarly, when you touch a hot stove, heat flows from the stove to your hand and your hand feels hot. It makes sense then that when a warm drink comes into contact with cold ice, heat will flow from the drink to the ice and the drink will become cooler.

Something very important also happens: The ice melts! Melting ice is an endothermic process. That is, the melting process absorbs heat from the surroundings causing the surroundings to cool off. It's the melting ice, not its cold temperature, that is most responsible for cooling the drink. The ability of ice to cool objects is largely due to the fact that some of the ice melts when it comes into contact with warm objects.

The heat change associated with melting ice or any other solid can be expressed quantitatively. The amount of heat absorbed from the surroundings when a specific amount of solid melts is called the *heat of fusion*. Heats of fusion are usually expressed in the SI units of kilojoules per mole (kJ/mol). The heat of fusion of ice is also commonly expressed in units of calories per gram (cal/g).

PURPOSE

In this lab, you will use the technique of calorimetry to measure the heat of fusion of ice, the amount of heat absorbed when ice melts. You will place a piece of ice into some hot water and record the temperature change of the system as the ice melts when energy flows from the hot water to the ice. You will first measure the mass and temperature of the hot water. You will also need to know the mass and temperature of the ice but, because of possible significant heat losses, you will determine these quantities indirectly. Because ice melts at 0°C, it will suffice to assume that the temperature of the ice is 0°C. To minimize heat loss, the best way to measure the mass of the ice is to measure the difference in mass of the hot water before and after you place the ice into it. You will carry out the experiment in an insulated polystyrene coffee cup.

Name _____ Class _____ Date _____

SAFETY 👓

- Wear your safety glasses.
- Use only small quantities for safety and cost efficiency.

MATERIALS

hot water from the tap
crushed ice

EQUIPMENT

alcohol thermometer
one-ounce plastic cup
polystyrene coffee cup
balance

EXPERIMENTAL PROCEDURE

1. Tare a polystyrene cup.

2. Fill a one-ounce plastic cup 1/4 full with hot water from the tap. Transfer it to the tared coffee cup and weigh it. Record the weight in Table 13.1.

3. Measure the temperature of the water and record it in Table 13.1.

4. Place a small ice chip into the water, stir and record in Table 13.1 the lowest temperature reached after the ice melts completely.

5. Reweigh the entire system and record your results in Table 13.1

6. Work through the calculations on the Experimental Data page and then repeat the experiment until your calculated heat of fusion of ice is consistent.

Name _____ Class _____ Date _____

EXPERIMENTAL DATA

Record your results in Tables 13.1 and 13.2 or tables like them in your notebook.

Table 13.1   Experimental Data

Quantity	Trial 1	Trial 2	Trial 3
a. Hot water weight (g)			
b. Hot water temperature (°C)			
c. Final temperature (°C)			
d. Total weight, hot water and ice (g)			
e. Ice Temperature (°C)			

Table 13.2   Calculated Data

Quantity	Calculation:	Trial 1	Trial 2	Trial 3
f. Ice weight (g)	d − a			
g. ΔT for hot water (°C)	c − b			
h. Heat lost by water (cal)	a × (c − b) × 1			
i. ΔT for ice (°C)	c − e			
j. Heat gained by ice (cal)	f × (c − e) × 1			
k. Heat lost + heat gained (cal)	h + j			
l. Heat of fusion of ice (cal/g)	−k/f			

CLEANING UP

Pour the water and ice down the drain. Recycle the cups. Put the thermometer away.

Name _____ Class _____ Date _____

QUESTIONS FOR ANALYSIS

Use what you learned in this lab to answer the following questions.

1. Without first weighing the ice, how can you tell the weight of the ice from your data?

   _____

   _____

2. Why is ΔT for the hot water negative? What does the negative sign mean?

   _____

   _____

   _____

   _____

3. What does the negative sign of the heat lost by the water signify?

   _____

   _____

4. Why can you assume the initial temperature of the ice is 0°C?

   _____

5. What is the sign of the heat absorbed by the ice? Explain.

   _____

6. The law of conservation of energy requires that the heat gained by the ice should balance the heat lost by the water assuming no losses of energy to the surroundings. Does item **k** in Table 13.2 of the calculated data equal zero? Explain.

   _____

   _____

   _____

7. Why does the heat required to melt the ice divided by the mass of the ice equal the heat of fusion of ice (heat of fusion = $-k/f$)? Why is the negative sign necessary?

   _____

   _____

   _____

8. Given that one calorie equals 4.18 joules, use your experimental data to calculate the heat of fusion of ice in joules per gram.

   _____

9. Use your experimental data to calculate the molar heat of fusion of ice in kJ/mol.

_____

10. Find the accepted value for the heat of fusion of ice in your textbook and compare your calculated values with the accepted value. Calculate a % error. % error = |experimental value − accepted value| × 100/accepted value.

_____

NOW IT'S YOUR TURN!

1. Try doing the experiment using a larger sample of hot water and ice. Use one ounce of hot water and about five times as much ice. Are your results similar? Explain.

_____

_____

2. Heat losses to the environment are an obvious source of error in this experiment. For example, significant heat losses can occur between the time you measure the temperature of the hot water and add the ice. Any cooling of the hot water during this period will result in an error. Analyze the experimental procedure and try to identify where it can be improved. Repeat the experiment using a modified method to optimize your results.

14 SYNTHESIS AND QUALITATIVE ANALYSIS OF GASES

Small-Scale Experiment for text section 12.1

OBJECTIVES

- **Carry out** chemical reactions that produce gases.
- **Detect** the aqueous reactions of gases using indicators.
- **Identify** unknown gases by the chemical reactions they undergo.

INTRODUCTION

Gases are found everywhere. Open a can or bottle of carbonated soft drink, and carbon dioxide, CO_2, bubbles appear. Balloons are commonly filled with helium, He. The gases that are undoubtedly the most familiar to us make up the atmosphere we breathe. Dry air is composed of approximately 78% nitrogen, N_2; 21% oxygen, O_2; and 1% argon, Ar. Usually air also contains considerable amounts of water vapor along with carbon dioxide and trace quantities of a wide variety of other gases. It is the oxygen in the air that sustains animal life, while carbon dioxide is essential to plant life.

Gases in the atmosphere have varying effects on our environment. Sulfur dioxide, SO_2, is produced from the burning of fuels like coal and oil that contain sulfur. Sulfur dioxide further oxidizes in the atmosphere to form sulfur trioxide, SO_3. Sulfur dioxide and sulfur trioxide are the major air pollutants responsible for acid rain. The oxides of nitrogen are a family of compounds commonly referred to as NO_x (NO_2, NO, N_2O_5, and N_2O). The presence of the NO_x family in the atmosphere is the trigger for photochemical smog. Carbon dioxide, CO_2, and water in the atmosphere are larger contributors to the greenhouse effect, enhanced global warming.

PURPOSE

In this lab you will investigate a variety of chemical reactions that produce gases. You will make each gas by mixing two aqueous solutions on a small-scale reaction surface. Different chemical reactions will produce different gases. You will cover the mixture with a clear plastic cup while the gas diffuses into an array of indicators placed around the mixture. You will study the color changes imparted to the indicators by the gases and learn to distinguish each gas by those color changes. Finally, you will identify unknown gases by the changes they impart to indicators.

SAFETY ⌾

- Wear your safety glasses.
- Use full small-scale pipets only for the carefully controlled delivery of liquids.

MATERIALS

Small-scale pipets of the following solutions:

hydrochloric acid (HCl)

potassium permanganate ($KMnO_4$)
sodium hypochlorite (NaOCl)
sodium hydroxide (NaOH)

sodium hydrogen sulfite ($NaHSO_3$)   sodium nitrite ($NaNO_2$)
sodium hydrogen carbonate ($NaHCO_3$)   hydrogen peroxide (H_2O_2)
ammonium chloride (NH_4Cl)   bromthymol blue (BTB)
potassium iodide (KI)   starch

EQUIPMENT

2 clear plastic cups
small-scale reaction surface

EXPERIMENTAL PAGE

1. Place 1 drop of each indicator solution in the squares near the inside edge of each circle. Mix 1 drop of each indicated solution in the center of each circle, and cover the entire circle with a cup. Be sure the cup does not touch any solutions.

2. Observe any changes that take place over several minutes. Also observe the nature of the gas bubbles (if any) produced by the mixing. Gases produced by the mixing of the reactants in the center will cause some of the indicators to change color. Record your results in Table 14.1.

3. Neutralize each of the mixtures in the centers with a few drops of NaOH; clean the reaction surface with a *damp* paper towel, and dry it. Clean the cups with a *dry* paper towel to absorb stray gases.

4. Repeat Step 3. Then turn over the Experimental Page and continue with the next mixing.

e. KI + starch | BTB | HCl + ☐ NaOCl | KI | KI + NaOCl + starch

f. KI + starch | BTB | NaOH + ☐ NH₄Cl | KI | KI + NaOCl + starch

5. Neutralize the mixtures in the centers with a few drops of NaOH each; clean the reaction surface with a *damp* paper towel, and dry it. Clean the cups with a *dry* paper towel to absorb stray gases.

Name _____ Class _____ Date _____

EXPERIMENTAL DATA

Record your results in Table 14.1 or a table like it in your notebook.

Table 14.1   Observations of Gases

Mixture	Bubbles?	BTB (Green)	KI + Starch (Colorless)	KI + NaOCl + Starch (Black)	KI (Colorless)
a. $NaHSO_3$ + HCl					
b. $NaNO_2$ + HCl					
c. $NaHCO_3$ + HCl					
d. H_2O_2 + $KMnO_4$					
e. NaOCl + HCl					
f. NH_4Cl + NaOH					

CLEANING UP

Avoid contamination by cleaning up in a way that protects you and your environment. Carefully clean the plastic cups by wiping them with a dry paper towel. Clean the small-scale reaction surface by absorbing the contents onto a paper towel, rinse the reaction surface with a damp paper towel, and dry it. Dispose of the paper towels in the waste bin. Wash your hands thoroughly with soap and water.

QUESTIONS FOR ANALYSIS

Use your Experimental Data and what you learned in this lab to answer the following questions.

1. What is unique about the way each gas behaved in the presence of indicators?

   _____

   _____

   _____

   _____

2. Gas d was oxygen. What evidence from your procedure might have led you to identify this gas as oxygen or nitrogen?

   _____

   _____

Name _____ Class _____ Date _____

3. Given the word equations below, write and balance chemical equations to describe the formation of each gas produced in the experiment:

a. Sodium hydrogen sulfite reacts with hydrochloric acid to produce sulfur dioxide gas, water, and sodium chloride.

_____

b. Sodium nitrite reacts with hydrochloric acid to produce nitrogen monoxide gas, water, sodium chloride, and sodium nitrate.

_____

Nitrogen monoxide gas from the above reaction reacts with oxygen gas in the air to produce nitrogen dioxide gas.

_____

c. Sodium hydrogen carbonate reacts with hydrochloric acid to produce carbon dioxide gas, water, and sodium chloride.

_____

d. Hydrogen peroxide reacts with permanganate ion and hydrogen ion to produce oxygen gas, manganese(II) ion, and water.

_____

e. Chlorine gas, water, and sodium chloride are produced when hydrochloric acid is added to sodium hypochlorite, NaOCl.

_____

f. Sodium hydroxide reacts with ammonium chloride to produce ammonia gas, water, and sodium chloride.

_____

4. Given the word equations below, write and balance chemical equations to describe each reaction of a gas with an indicator or the water in the indicator. In each case explain the change in the indicator. The letter of each word equation corresponds to the letter on the Experimental Page where you saw that reaction.

a. Sulfur dioxide gas reacts with water in the BTB indicator to produce sulfurous acid. (Hint: The formula for sulfurous acid has one fewer oxygen atom than the formula for sulfuric acid.)

_____

Sulfur dioxide gas also reacts with iodine and water to form iodide ion, sulfate ion, and hydrogen ion.

_____

_____

b. Nitrogen dioxide gas reacts with water in the indicator to produce nitric acid and nitrous acid.

_____

c. Chlorine gas reacts with iodide ion to form iodine and chloride ion.

_____

_____

Chlorine gas also reacts with water in BTB to form hydrochloric acid and hypochlorous acid.

_____

d. Ammonia gas reacts with water in the BTB indicator to produce hydroxide ion and ammonium ion.

_____

NOW IT'S YOUR TURN!

1. Obtain six unknown solutions from your instructor and apply the technique you used in this experiment to identify the unknown solutions and the gases they produce. Make a table of the number and formula of each solution and each unknown gas it produces.

_____

_____

2. Acids like ethanoic acid, CH_3COOH, and hydrochloric acid, HCl, are appreciably volatile. That is, they readily evaporate from solution. Design and carry out a way of detecting aqueous solutions of these acids by using this gas detection method. Can your method distinguish these acids from sulfuric and nitric acids? Can it distinguish these acids from one another?

_____

_____

_____

_____

3. Besides oxygen, your breath contains carbon dioxide and water vapor. This is because all animals use oxygen to metabolize sugar molecules in a process called cell respiration. The products are CO_2 and H_2O:

$$C_6H_{12}O_6 + 6O_2 \rightarrow 6CO_2 + 6H_2O$$

Carbon dioxide reacts with water to produce carbonic acid, H_2CO_3. Write a balanced equation for this reaction. Using this reaction, devise a way to detect CO_2 in your breath. **Caution:** *Do not touch your mouth to any chemicals or to any apparatus!*

_____

_____

_____

15 DESIGN AND CONSTRUCTION OF A QUANTITATIVE SPECTROSCOPE

Small-Scale Experiment for text section 13.3

OBJECTIVES

- **Design** and **construct** a quantitative spectroscope.
- **Build** a device to calibrate the spectroscope.

INTRODUCTION

Chemistry is used to solve problems by identifying materials. Criminologists solve crimes by identifying minute quantities of blood, soil, paint, and other materials that link the criminal with the crime. Radio astronomers identify molecules in outer space. Chemists routinely detect and identify pollutants in our air, water, and soil. Most often these identifications are made by using some form of spectroscopic analysis, or spectroscopy. Spectroscopy is a term that describes a wide range of chemical analyses that probe the interaction of light with matter. Many spectroscopic instruments have been developed to measure different features of light as it interacts with matter.

Perhaps the most obvious feature of visible light is color. When white light from a lamp or the sun travels through a drop of water, it is dispersed into its component colors. This familiar rainbow of colors is known as the visible spectrum. You can produce the same effect by passing light through a prism or diffraction grating. By investigating the visible spectra of various light sources, you can learn about how light interacts with matter.

PURPOSE

In this lab you will design and build a spectroscope, a device with which you can observe the spectra of various light sources. The body of the spectroscope will be a rectangular box, about 2 cm thick, made from dark-colored poster board. The spectroscope will have a narrow slit at one end to allow light to enter it. A diffraction grating at the other end will disperse white light into a spectrum by bending it at different angles. You should make the box relatively "light-tight" except for the slit and the diffraction grating. Finally, you will build a device to calibrate the spectroscope by taking advantage of a principle called total internal reflection. You will use a plastic rod to "pipe" light into the spectroscope box. A grid scratched on the rod will scatter light and appear to glow inside the box.

SAFETY 🥽

- Behave in a way that is consistent with a safe laboratory.
- Do not look directly at sunlight with your eyes or with the spectroscope. Look at the bright sky away from the sun or at the sun's reflection off snow or a sidewalk.
- Keep all electrical light sources away from water, water faucets, and sinks.

EQUIPMENT

teacher-built spectroscope
poster board
diffraction grating
tape
adhesive labels

plastic light rod
scissors
3 rubber bands
ruler and 2-cm guide strip
nail

EXPERIMENTAL PROCEDURE

Part A. The Structure and Function of a Spectroscope

1. Hold a slide-mounted diffraction grating up to your eye and look at a light source. Be careful not to touch the plastic surface of the grating with your fingers. Record what you see.

2. Look at the plastic surface of the grating. Again, don't touch the plastic! Record what you see.

3. Look through the teacher-built spectroscope (without a diffraction grating) at a light source. Record what you see.

4. Place the slide-mounted diffraction grating over the square hole in the teacher-built spectroscope. Hold the grating and spectroscope up to your eye and look through it at a light source. Record what you see.

5. Look through the spectroscope with both your left and right eyes. Record similarities and differences.

Part B. Building Your Own Spectroscope

6. Use a guide strip to draw a 2-cm-wide border around a piece of poster board. Draw a 2-cm-wide center strip as shown in Figure 15.1.

Figure 15.1 *The body of the spectroscope showing folds and cuts*

7. Cut out the diagonal corners entirely as shown. Cut out the four slits 0.5 cm wide and 1 cm from each indicated edge.

8. Use the straight edge of a ruler and fold the poster board along all the lighter lines to form a rectangular box. The slits should line up when the poster board is folded. If they don't, simply cut the poster board so they do. Use rubber bands to hold the folded spectroscope together.

9. Tape a small rectangle of diffraction grating over one slit. Then tape two small pieces of poster board over the other slit to make it 2 mm wide. Take care not to touch the diffraction grating.

10. Place the plastic light rod over the template in Figure 15.2. Use the template as a guide, and use a nail to carefully trace a grid onto the light rod. First trace the horizontal scratch and then the evenly spaced parallel scratches onto the light rod.

Figure 15.2 *Template for tracing grid onto light rod*

11. Slide the light rod into the end of the spectroscope opposite the diffraction grating (Figure 15.3), and look through it at a white light source. What do you see?

Figure 15.3 *Positioning of the light rod in the spectroscope*

12. When you're sure everything is square and lines up correctly, tape the box together so it's "light tight."

Name _____ Class _____ Date _____

EXPERIMENTAL DATA

Part A. Record your data as you examine the spectroscope.

1. What do you see when you hold a slide-mounted diffraction grating up to your eye?

   _____

2. What do you see on the plastic surface of the grating?

   _____

3. What do you see when you look through the teacher-built spectroscope at a light source?

   _____

4. What colors do you see and in what order are they when you add the slide-mounted diffraction grating?

   _____

5. Do the colors appear in the same order when you look to the left of the slit as opposed to the right of the slit?

   _____

Part B. Building your own spectroscope.

6. Draw a picture of your completed spectroscope.

7. What do you see when you look through the completed spectroscope?

   _____

CLEANING UP

Label your spectroscope with your name. Clean up all scraps of paper. Please recycle all usable materials.

QUESTIONS FOR ANALYSIS

Use what you learned in this lab to answer the following questions.

1. What is a spectroscope?

    _____

2. What is a spectrum?

    _____

3. What is white light? How do you know?

    _____

    _____

4. Which part of the spectroscope separates light into its component colors?

    _____

5. What are the colors of the visible spectrum?

    _____

6. How does the light rod work?

    _____

    _____

NOW IT'S YOUR TURN!

1. Try using various boxes to build spectroscopes. Try a shoe box, a cracker box, a safety-glasses box, a toothpaste box, a pizza box, a cereal box, or any other box available to you. Design each spectroscope so that you can use the same diffraction grating interchangeably.

2. Investigate new ways to calibrate the spectroscope using various light rods.

3. Investigate the effect of changing the size and shape of the slit on your spectroscope.

16 VISIBLE SPECTRA AND THE NATURE OF LIGHT AND COLOR

Small-Scale Experiment for text section 13.3

OBJECTIVES

- **Calibrate** a quantitative spectroscope.
- **Compare** visible spectra of common light sources, using a quantitative spectroscope.
- **Plot** graphic representations of various visible spectra.
- **Measure** the wavelength of any colored line in the visible spectrum, and **identify** the range of wavelengths that comprise each color.

INTRODUCTION

The diffraction grating in a spectroscope breaks white light into a series of colors called the *visible spectrum*. The visible spectrum is the entire range of colors your eyes can see. A quick look through the spectroscope you built in Small-Scale Experiment 15 will show you that visible white light is a mixture of all colors of the rainbow.

When you look at fluorescent light, three very prominent lines or narrow bands of bright color are superimposed on this continuous rainbow. One line is *violet*; one is *green*; and one is *yellow*. These three lines are caused by the light emission of glowing gaseous mercury atoms in the fluorescent tube. The lines all have characteristic specific positions in the visible spectrum, or *wavelengths*, measured in nanometers (nm):

violet – 436 nm   green – 546 nm   yellow – 580 nm

PURPOSE

In this lab you will use the characteristic wavelength of the prominent spectral lines of mercury to calibrate your spectroscope. The spectroscope contains a plastic light rod that you will use to mark the positions of mercury emission lines. Scratches on the rod appear to glow inside the box. You can use the lighted ruler to mark any place on the visible spectrum. You will move the light rod so that the longest lighted scratch on the ruler is centered over the prominent violet line of the spectrum. You will then note the positions of the other lines on the ruler. These positions are related to the corresponding wavelengths of the prominent lines. Once you have identified the positions of two of the three lines for which you know the wavelength in nanometers, you can calculate the number of nanometers each graduation on the grid represents. The entire process is called *calibration*.

You can then measure any wavelength of visible light in nanometers, represented by the scratches. All you have to do is note the place on the spectrum you wish to know and compare it to the grid you have scratched out on the light rod.

SAFETY

- Behave in a way that is consistent with a safe laboratory.
- Do not look directly at sunlight with the spectroscope. Look at a bright sky away from the sun or at the sun's reflection off snow or a sidewalk.
- Keep all electrical light sources away from water, water faucets, and sinks.

EQUIPMENT

spectroscope
fluorescent and incandescent light sources
graph paper

EXPERIMENTAL PROCEDURE

Part A. Calibrating the Spectroscope

1. View the visible spectrum (rainbow) of fluorescent light through your spectroscope. Identify the three prominent colored lines or narrow bands of brightly colored light superimposed on the rainbow (violet, green, and yellow). Make a rough sketch of the rainbow with its three most prominent bands in your Experimental Data.

2. Move the plastic light rod so that the longest parallel scratch is exactly superimposed over the center of the prominent violet line in the spectrum. Fix the position of the rod with tape, if necessary. The spectroscope is now calibrated.

3. Find the center of the green line relative to the violet line by counting the number of spaces between scratches that separate them. (If this is not a whole number of spaces, estimate the fraction of space.) Repeat for the center of the more diffuse yellow line.

4. Draw in the positions of the green and yellow lines on Figure 16.1 of the Experimental Data section.

Part B. The Visible Spectrum of Fluorescent Light

5. Look through your spectroscope at fluorescent light again.

   a. Note and record the position in spaces from the violet line that marks the *outer edge of the red* region of the spectrum (where red meets black).

   b. Note and record the position of the spectrum where *red meets orange*. This is not very distinct. There is a gradual change from red to orange. Make your own judgement!

   c. Note and record the other places on the spectrum where one color appears to fade into another. Use your judgement!

   d. Use your data to plot a visible spectrum of *fluorescent light* in the Experimental Data section. Find the point on the calibration grid that corresponds to each position of the mark. Read the wavelength that corresponds to that point.

6. Use your spectroscope and the same calibration grid to plot the visible spectrum of *incandescent light* (light from an overhead projector reflected off a white wall or screen, for example).

EXPERIMENTAL DATA

Part A. Calibrating a Spectroscope

1. Make a rough sketch of the rainbow produced from fluorescent light, clearly showing the three prominent colored lines or bands of light (violet, green, and yellow).

2. Superimpose the light rod on your drawing, showing the approximate positions of the scratches.

3. How many spaces from the violet line is the green line? The yellow line?

_____

_____

4. The grid shown in Figure 16.1 below is a representation of the grid on the light rod. The violet line is superimposed on the longest scratch.

   a. Draw in the positions of the green and yellow lines with their wavelengths.

   b. Find how many nanometers each small graduation represents by dividing the difference in wavelengths of the green and violet lines (538 − 436 = 102 nm) by the number of spaces between them. Mark the grid in nanometers.

_____

Part B. The Visible Spectrum of Fluorescent Light

5. Plot the spectrum of fluorescent light.

6. Plot the spectrum of incandescent light.

CLEANING UP

Put all the equipment back in its proper place.

QUESTIONS FOR ANALYSIS

1. Explain why the scratched grid on the rod appears to glow.

   _____

   _____

2. What part of the spectroscope separates white light into its component colors?

   _____

3. For each of the spectra you plotted, name the colors in the order they appear, and state the wavelengths that border each color.

   _____

   _____

   _____

   _____

4. Compare the plots of the visible spectra of fluorescent and incandescent light. Point out the similarities and differences of each. Which source of light has more red in it? Which has more blue?

   _____

5. Which color forms the widest band in each spectrum?

   _____

6. Why does the incandescent light have the three prominent colored lines in it?

_____

_____

7. Why does each different spectroscope need to be calibrated?

_____

NOW IT'S YOUR TURN!

1. Use your spectroscope and a calibration grid like Figure 16.1 to plot the visible spectra of two other light sources: candlelight and sunlight. Don't look directly at the sunlight! Look away from the sun at a bright sky or at sunlight reflected off snow or a sidewalk. How are sunlight and candlelight the same? How are they different?

_____

_____

2. A *reflectance spectrum* is the spectrum of light that is reflected off an opaque object from a source of white light. Use your spectroscope and the same calibration grid to plot the *visible reflection* of various colors of construction paper. What interesting observations do you make?

3. An *absorption spectrum* is the spectrum of light that is transmitted through a translucent material like a colored solution or plastic film. Measure the absorption spectra of several colored plastic films. What can you conclude about the colors your eye perceives and the actual colors of light passing through the films?

4. Measure the absorption spectra of various colored solutions. Use the fluorescent light box to place behind the solutions. What can you conclude about the colors your eye perceives and the actual colors of light passing through the colored solutions?

5. An *atomic emission spectrum* is the spectrum that is emitted from glowing gaseous atoms. Examine the atomic emission spectra of several gas discharge tubes. Make a rough sketch of each in your notebook. What is distinctive about all these atomic emission spectra?

6. Propose how you can make the spectroscope better. Reinvent it. Build another model and test its performance based on various construction parameters.

7. The wavelength of light is the distance between two adjacent peaks of a light wave. The wavelength of visible light is most commonly measured in nanometers (nm). One nanometer is 10^{-9} meters. The frequency of light is the number of waves passing a given point in 1 second. Its units are s^{-1}. The velocity of light in a vacuum is about 3×10^8 meters/second. The wavelength, frequency, and speed of light are related in terms of the following equation:

$$\text{frequency} = \text{velocity}/\text{wavelength} \quad \nu = c/\lambda$$

Choose any visible spectrum you plotted and use the above equation to convert all the measured wavelengths into frequencies.

8. Mix equal quantities of red, blue, and yellow food dyes in all possible binary combinations (any one with any other one.) What do you conclude?

_____

_____

_____

17 HALOGEN IONS IN SOLUTION

Small-Scale Experiment for text section 14.2

OBJECTIVES

- **Observe** the chemical properties of halide ions in aqueous solution.
- **Identify** halide ions by noting the differences in their chemical properties.
- **Describe** the chemical reactions of halide ions by writing and balancing chemical and net ionic equations.

INTRODUCTION

Halogens is the name given to the family of elements that comprise Group 17 (VIIA), on the periodic table. The individual elements are fluorine, chlorine, bromine, iodine, and astatine. All but astatine are relatively common elements. Because they are chemically reactive, the halogens never occur as single, free atoms in nature. The halogens form a large number of compounds and have many uses. In the elemental form, halogens are most stable as diatomic molecules whose formulas are written F_2, Cl_2, Br_2, and I_2.

The reactivity of the halogens and their similar properties are due to their very similar electron configurations. All halogens have seven valence (outer orbital) electrons, and each halogen readily gains one electron to form an anion with a single negative charge:

$$X + e^- \rightarrow X \qquad \text{where } X = F, Cl, Br, I$$

These halogen anions are called halide ions. Their individual names are derived from their element names: F^- = fluoride, Cl^- = chloride, Br^- = bromide, and I^- = iodide.

PURPOSE

In this lab you will examine some of the chemical reactions of the halide ions, derived from the halogen elements. You will learn to write chemical equations to describe their reactions. You will learn to use these chemical reactions to distinguish one halide ion from another.

SAFETY

- Wear your safety glasses.
- Use full small-scale pipets only for the carefully controlled delivery of liquids.

MATERIALS

Small-scale pipets of the following solutions:

calcium chloride ($CaCl_2$)	potassium fluoride (KF)
potassium chloride (KCl)	potassium bromide (KBr)
ammonia (NH_3)	sodium thiosulfate ($Na_2S_2O_3$)
starch	bromothymol blue (BTB)
iron(III) chloride ($FeCl_3$)	potassium iodide (KI)
FD&C blue #1 (blue dye)	hydrogen peroxide (H_2O_2)

lead(II) nitrate ($Pb(NO_3)_2$)
silver nitrate ($AgNO_3$)
sodium hypochlorite (NaOCl)
copper(II) sulfate ($CuSO_4$)

hydrochloric acid (HCl)

EQUIPMENT

small-scale reaction surface
empty pipet for stirring
clear plastic cup

EXPERIMENTAL PAGE

Part A. Chemistry of the Halide Ions

1. Add 1 drop of each of the indicated solutions on the **X**. Stir each mixture by blowing air with an empty small-scale pipet. Record your results in Table 17.1.

	KF (F$^-$)	KCl (Cl$^-$)	KBr (Br$^-$)	KI (I$^-$)	
a. CaCl$_2$ (Ca^{2+})	X	X	X	X	
b. Pb(NO$_3$)$_2$ (Pb^{2+})	X	X	X	X	
c. AgNO$_3$ (Ag$^+$)	X	X	X	X	Now add 5–10 drops NH$_3$ to each and stir. Look for a change.
d. AgNO$_3$ (Ag$^+$)	X	X	X	X	Now add 5–10 drops Na$_2$S$_2$O$_3$ to each and stir. Look for a change.
e. NaOCl (OCl$^-$)	X	X	X	X	Now add 1 drop of starch and 1 drop of HCl to each and stir. Look for a change.

Part B. Chemistry of Chlorine Gas, Cl$_2$(g)

2. Place 1 drop of each solution in the indicated space. Add 1 drop of NaOCl to the HCl and cover the entire array with a cup. Observe the drops for any change over time, about 10 minutes. After you record your results in Table 17.2, turn this page over and continue the experiment.

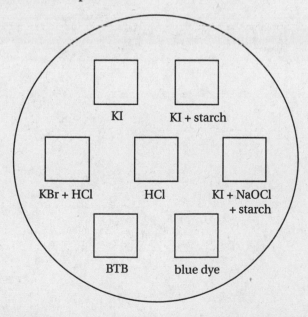

Part C. Chemistry of the Iodide Ion

3. Mix 1 drop of each of the following solutions on the **X**'s. Record your results in Table 17.3.

	NaOCl	CuSO$_4$	FeCl$_3$	H$_2$O$_2$
Kl	**X**	**X**	**X**	**X**

Now add 1 drop of starch to each mixture, then 1 drop of HCl.

EXPERIMENTAL DATA

Record your results in Tables 17.1, 17.2, and 17.3 or tables like them in your notebook.

Table 17.1   Chemistry of the Halide Ions

	KF (F^-)	KCl (Cl^-)	KBr (Br^-)	KI (I^-)	
a. $CaCl_2$ (Ca^{2+})					
b. $Pb(NO_3)_2$ (Pb^{2+})					
c. $AgNO_3$ (Ag^+)					
d. $AgNO_3$ (Ag^+)					
e. NaOCl (OCl^-)					

Table 17.2   Chemistry of Chlorine Gas, $Cl_2(g)$

	KI colorless	KBr + HCl colorless	BTB green	KI + starch colorless	blue dye blue	Starch + KI + NaOCl black
HCl + NaOCl						

Table 17.3   Chemistry of Iodide Ion

	NaOCl	$CuSO_4$	$FeCl_3$	H_2O_2
KI				

Name _____ Class _____ Date _____

CLEANING UP

Avoid contamination by cleaning up in a way that protects you and your environment. Carefully clean the reaction surface by absorbing the contents onto a paper towel. Rinse the reaction surface with a damp paper towel and dry it. Clean the plastic cup by wiping it with a dry paper towel. Dispose of the paper towels in the waste bin. Wash your hands thoroughly with soap and water.

QUESTIONS FOR ANALYSIS

Use what you have learned in this lab to answer the following questions.

1. What similarities did you observe in the reactions of halogens in Part A?

   _____

2. Describe how the four halide ions—F^-, Cl^-, Br^-, and I^-—can be distinguished from one another. (That is, what chemical solutions undergo reactions that are unique to each ion?

   _____

   _____

3. Lead(II) ion reacts with iodide ion to produce a lead(II) iodide precipitate:

   $$Pb^{2+} + 2I^- \rightarrow PbI_2(s)$$

   Write similar net ionic equations to describe the other precipitation reactions you observed.

   _____   _____

   _____   _____

   _____   _____

4. Would you get different results if you used aqueous solutions of sodium halides rather than potassium halides? Explain.

   _____

   _____

5. Silver forms a *complex* ion with ammonia:

   $$AgX(s) + 2NH_3 \rightarrow Ag(NH_3)_2^+ + X^-$$

   In the equation above, X represents a halide ion. Write equations for the reactions of ammonia for the silver halides that dissolve in ammonia by replacing X with each halide ion that dissolves.

   _____

   _____

   _____

6. Silver halide precipitates also dissove in excess thiosulfate, $S_2O_3^{2-}$, to form the complex ion $Ag(S_2O_3)_2^{3-}$.

$$AgX(s) + 2S_2O_3^{2-} \rightarrow Ag(S_2O_3)_2^{3-} + X^-$$

Write equations for each reaction you observed with thiosulfate.

_____

_____

7. The reaction of iodide ion, I^-, with NaOCl can be described by the following equation:

$$OCl^- + 2H^+ + 2I^- \rightarrow Cl^- + I_2 + HOH$$

Write an equation for the reaction of bromide ion with NaOCl.

_____

8. Which chemical product in the sample equation in Question 7 is responsible for the formation of the black color with starch?

_____

9. Describe in your own words what must have happened under the cup to cause reactions in the solutions without mixing them with any other solution.

_____

_____

10. Sodium hypochlorite, NaOCl, reacts with hydrochloric acid to yield chlorine gas, sodium chloride, and water. Write the chemical equation.

_____

11. Given the word equation, write a balanced chemical equation to describe each reaction between chlorine gas and the indicated reagent. In each case, explain the change in the reagent.

a. Chlorine gas reacts with water to produce hydrochloric acid and hypochlorous acid, HOCl.

_____

_____

b. Chlorine reacts with iodide ion to form iodine and chloride ion.

_____

_____

c. Chlorine reacts similarly with bromide ion.

_____

12. What color do all the reaction mixtures in Part C have in common? What chemical species is indicated by this color?

_____

13. Write and balance chemical equations for all the reactions you observed in Part C. Here are some hints.

$Cl_2 + I^- \rightarrow Cl^- + ?$ _____

$Cu^{2+} + I^- \rightarrow CuI(s) + ?$ _____

$Fe^{3+} + I^- \rightarrow Fe^{2+} + ?$ _____

$H_2O_2 + I^- + H^+ \rightarrow H_2O + ?$ _____

NOW IT'S YOUR TURN!

1. Study the chemistry of bromine, Br_2, by setting up KI, KI + starch, and BTB indicators like those in Part B. Instead of using NaOCl and HCl in the center, use 1 drop each of the following: KBr, KIO_3, and HCl. The reaction is

$$6Br^- + IO_3^- + 6H^+ \rightarrow 3Br_2 + I^- + 3H_2O$$

Report the results of each mixing. Complete and balance the following chemical equations. (Hint: They are like the reactions of Cl_2.)

$Br_2 + I^- \rightarrow$ $Br_2 + H_2O \rightarrow$

$Br_2 + 2I^- \rightarrow 2Br^- + I_2$ $Br_2 + H_2O \rightarrow HBr + HOBr$

	KI colorless	KI + starch colorless	BTB green
$HCl + KBr + KIO_3$			

2. Both I_2 and Br_2 are nonpolar molecules. This means that they are more soluble in nonpolar solvents like baby oil than they are in polar solvents like water. On the other hand, I^- and Br^- are water-soluble ions. Use aqueous solutions of I^- and Br^- to generate some I_2 and Br_2, and watch them dissolve in a non-polar solvent like baby oil. On a glass slide, mix 1 drop of each of the following:

	KI + HCl	KBr + HCl
NaOCl + baby oil	+	+

Observe over time. Write chemical equations for each reaction. What color does each halogen appear to be in the baby oil?

_____

_____

_____

18 HARD AND SOFT WATER

Small-Scale Experiment for text section 15.2

OBJECTIVES

- **Measure** the total hardness of water in various water samples.
- **Apply** the ion exchange process to "soften" hard water.

INTRODUCTION

Hard water contains dissolved salts, especially those of calcium. Hard water often contains magnesium and iron ions also. Most of the dissolved calcium ions in the natural waters of rivers, lakes, and streams originate from limestone, which is principally calcium carbonate, $CaCO_3$. The limestone is dissolved by rain water or by water contaminated by mining and industrial wastes containing hydrochloric and sulfuric acids.

$$CaCO_3(s) + H^+(aq) \rightarrow Ca^{2+}(aq) + HCO_3^-(aq)$$

The reaction of water with atmospheric carbon dioxide makes rain water naturally slightly acidic. Unnatural acidic rain can result from the reaction of atmospheric water with industrial pollutants like sulfur dioxide and nitrogen dioxide.

$$H_2O + CO_2(g) \rightarrow H_2CO_3(aq)$$
$$H_2O + SO_2(g) \rightarrow H_2SO_3(aq)$$
$$H_2O + 2NO_2(g) \rightarrow HNO_2(aq) + HNO_3(aq)$$

The location of limestone deposits varies throughout the country, as do the amounts of industrial acids exposed to rivers and the acidity of rainfall. Thus, the amount of dissolved calcium ion varies, and so does the resultant hardness of water in various locations.

Calcium ions, while nontoxic, present a number of significant household and industrial problems. For example, calcium ion reacts with the ingredients of many soaps and shampoos to form an insoluble scum that you know as a "bath tub ring." The formation of this precipitate causes the soap to lose its effectiveness.

$$Ca^{2+} + 2CH_3(CH_2)_{15}COO^- \, Na^+ \rightarrow 2Na^+ + (CH_3(CH_2)_{15}COO^-)_2Ca(s)$$

           sodium stearate   calcium stearate
           a typical soap   an insoluble scum

Hard water also accounts for the buildup of "boiler scale" on the insides of teapots, water heaters, and industrial boilers. The scale consists mainly of calcium carbonate that has precipitated from hard water upon heating:

$$Ca(HCO_3)_2(aq) + heat \rightarrow CaCO_3(s) + CO_2(g) + H_2O$$

The calcium carbonate scale must be removed periodically because it reduces heating efficiency by acting as an insulator. Calcium carbonate also promotes corrosion and blocks pipes.

PURPOSE

In this lab you will measure the total amount of calcium and magnesium ions in various water samples from around the country and/or from your area. You will add a particular kind of solution, called a buffer, to each water sample which will maintain the pH at about 10.5. You will then titrate each sample with ethylenediamine tetraacetic acid, EDTA, until the indicator Ero-T turns from wine red to sky blue at the end point.

You will report the results as parts per million (ppm) of calcium carbonate, $CaCO_3$, even though some of the hardness may be due to the presence of magnesium ions. A part per million is a milligram of calcium carbonate per liter of water sample. The higher the parts per million of $CaCO_3$, the more calcium ions are in the water and the harder the water is.

SAFETY 👓

- Wear your safety glasses.
- Use full small-scale pipets only for the carefully controlled delivery of liquids.

MATERIALS

Small-scale pipets of the following solutions:

ethylenediamine tetraacetic acid (EDTA)	ammonia/ammonium chloride (buffer)
deionized water (H_2O)	various water samples (labeled)
Solids: eriochrome black T indicator (Ero-T)	

EQUIPMENT

small-scale balance with extra pan or other balance

EXPERIMENTAL PROCEDURE

Determine the hardness of each water sample by the following method:

1. Weigh about 2500 mg of water sample in a plastic cup.

   a. Place a 2500 mg weight in your small-scale balance pan, and adjust the balance beam and counterweight until the pointer indicates the zero point.

   b. Remove the weight and drop in enough water sample to return the pointer to the zero point.

2. Add 15 drops of buffer.

3. Add Ero-T indicator until the color is medium to dark wine red.

4. Weigh or tare a full pipet of EDTA.

   a. Place a full pipet in a second small-scale balance pan.

   b. Adjust the small-scale balance to read zero.

5. Titrate the water sample with EDTA until the last tinges of red turn blue.

6. Find the weight loss of EDTA.

    a. Return the used EDTA pipet to the small-scale balance.

    b. Add weights until the pointer again reads zero.

7. Repeat the above steps for each of the other water samples including one from your tap and distilled water. Compare the hardness of water in the various other samples available in your lab.

8. Calculate the parts per million (ppm) of $CaCO_3$ in the water sample. (1 ppm = 1 mg $CaCO_3$/L of water.) Record your results in Table 18.1. To do the calculation you will need the following pieces of information:

    a. The weight loss of EDTA used in the titration in mg.

    b. The weight of the water sample in mg.

    c. The density of EDTA solution = 1000 mg/1 mL.

    d. The density of water = 1000 mg/1 mL.

    e. 1000 mL/1 L.

    f. The concentration of EDTA solution = 0.002 mmol/mL.

    g. The overall stoichiometry of the reaction = 1 mmol $CaCO_3$/1 mmol EDTA.

    h. The formula weight of $CaCO_3$ = 100 mg/mmol.

$$\text{ppm } CaCO_3 = \text{mg } CaCO_3/\text{L } H_2O = \frac{\mathbf{a}}{\mathbf{b}} \times \frac{\mathbf{d}}{\mathbf{c}} \times \mathbf{e} \times \mathbf{f} \times \mathbf{g} \times \mathbf{h}$$

To be sure you understand the calculation, substitute each quantity (number and units) into the equation and cancel the units. For subsequent calculations, simplify the equation by combining terms that are always constant.

The indicator is red in the presence of Mg^{2+}. EDTA reacts with both Ca^{2+} and Mg^{2+}. The indicator turns blue when all of the Mg^{2+} and Ca^{2+} are combined with EDTA.

Equations:

$$Mg^{2+} + 2In^- = MgIn_2 \qquad\qquad EDTA^{2-} + Ca^{2+} \rightarrow CaEDTA$$

$$\text{blue} \qquad\qquad \text{red} \qquad\qquad\qquad EDTA^{2-} + Mg^{2+} \rightarrow MgEDTA$$

Name _____ Class _____ Date _____

EXPERIMENTAL DATA

Record your results in Table 18.1 or a table like it in your notebook.

Table 18.1   Titration Data for Water Samples

Water Sample	Sample Weight (mg)	Weight Loss of EDTA (mg)	ppm CaCO$_3$

CLEANING UP

Avoid contamination by cleaning up in a way that protects you and your environment. Carefully clean the plastic balance cup by rinsing the contents down the drain. Rinse the cup and dry it with a paper towel. Dispose of the paper towels in the waste bin. Wash your hands thoroughly with soap and water.

QUESTIONS FOR ANALYSIS

Use what you learned in this lab to answer the following questions.

1. Which sample is the hardest water you titrated? Which is the softest? What does it mean for water to be "hard" or "soft"?

_____

_____

_____

2. What is a part per million?

_____

3. In the titration, why did you not need to know the weight of the full EDTA pipet?

_____

4. Write a balanced equation for the titration of calcium ion with EDTA.

_____

5. EDTA is commonly used as an additive in foods such as salad dressings and carbonated soft drinks. The function of the EDTA is to tie up metal cations that may cause clouding of the product. Read some labels at home and find some foods that contain EDTA in some form. List them here.

_____

NOW IT'S YOUR TURN!

1. When water is passed through an ion exchange buret, it becomes acidic because Ca^+ ions are exchanged for H^+ ions. The equation for the ion exchange reaction follows:

$$Ca^{2+} + H^+H^+ \rightarrow Ca^{2+} + 2H^+$$

$$\begin{array}{cc} \backslash \diagup & | \\ R & R \end{array} \qquad R = \text{ion exchange "resin"}$$

This principle is used in a practical everyday setting in a home water softener.

a. Recharge an acid resin ion exchanger with a small amount of HCl.

b. Drain it thoroughly and rinse it twice with deionized water. Expel as much of the rinse water as possible.

c. Draw a few drops of hard water into the exchanger and shake gently for 15 seconds. Add 5 drops of this water to 1 drop of BTB and record the color. What color does each water sample that was treated in the ion exchanger turn BTB? What ions are present in these samples?

_____

d. Expel 5 more drops from the exchanger, shake in a few grains of Ero-T indicator and add a few drops of buffer. Record the color.

e. Repeat for the other water samples. What color does each water sample that was treated with the ion exchanger turn Ero-T? What does this tell you about the presence of calcium ion? Explain.

_____

_____

REACTIONS OF AQUEOUS IONIC COMPOUNDS

Small-Scale Experiment for text section 15.2

OBJECTIVES

- **Observe** a large number of chemical reactions by mixing solutions of ionic compounds.
- **Classify** a large amount of data efficiently, using a matrix.
- **Identify** unknown chemicals by using information in the data matrix.

INTRODUCTION

Science progresses through the process of experimentation: *asking questions, finding ways to answer them, and generating more questions.* As a student of chemistry you make many observations in the process of designing and carrying out experiments. You organize your observations in tables so that they are clearly available for answering questions and solving problems. Then you can compare your well-organized data in order to answer questions and solve problems. You consider all the data so you can make correlations that would not be possible if each observation were considered alone. Your correlations may raise more questions than they answer. But these new questions promote further experimentation which raises more answers and more questions.

All of the steps in the process of experimentation depend on your carefully made observations. The prerequisite to answering any chemical question or to solving any chemical problem is the accumulation of sufficient, accurate, and well-organized observations.

PURPOSE

In this lab you will solve a chemical logic problem. You will mix 13 solutions of known ionic compounds in all possible binary (two at a time) combinations. You will record your observations in such a way that comparisons of the chemical behavior of the various mixtures can be made easily. You will study the similarities and differences between the reactions of ionic compounds, and you will use your record of observations to determine the identity of various unknown solutions. In Small-Scale Experiment 20, you will use the data obtained in this experiment to identify eight unknown solutions chosen at random from the original 13.

SAFETY

- Wear your safety glasses.
- Use full small-scale pipets only for the carefully controlled delivery of liquids.

MATERIALS

Small-scale pipets of the following solutions:

ammonia (NH_3)
calcium chloride ($CaCl_2$)
sodium phosphate (Na_3PO_4)

sodium carbonate (Na_2CO_3)
potassium iodide (KI)
iron(III) chloride ($FeCl_3$)

copper(II) sulfate ($CuSO_4$)
lead(II) nitrate ($Pb(NO_3)_2$)
silver nitrate ($AgNO_3$)
sodium hydroxide (NaOH)

hydrochloric acid (HCl)
sulfuric acid (H_2SO_4)
nitric acid (HNO_3)

EQUIPMENT

small-scale reaction surface
empty pipet for stirring

EXPERIMENTAL PAGE

Place 1 drop of $Pb(NO_3)_2$ on each X in the first column. Add 1 drop of each of the other solutions to the $Pb(NO_3)_2$. Stir each mixture by blowing air with an empty pipet. Repeat the procedure for each column. Record your results in Table 19.1.

Place this side of the Experimental Page facedown. Use the other side under your small-scale reaction surface.

Name _____ Class _____ Date _____

EXPERIMENTAL DATA

Record your results in Table 19.1 or a table like it in your notebook.

Table 19.1   Reactions of Aqueous Ionic Compounds

Name _____ Class _____ Date _____

CLEANING UP

Avoid contamination by cleaning up in a way that protects you and your environment. Carefully clean the small-scale reaction surface by absorbing the contents onto a paper towel. Rinse the reaction surface with a damp paper towel and dry it. Dispose of the paper towels in the waste bin. Wash your hands thoroughly with soap and water.

QUESTIONS FOR ANALYSIS

Use what you learned in this lab to answer the following questions.

1. Write and balance chemical equations for each precipitation reaction you observed for lead(II) nitrate. For example, lead(II) nitrate, $Pb(NO_3)_2$, and potassium iodide, KI, react to form a very bright yellow precipitate:

$$Pb(NO_3)_2 + 2KI \rightarrow PbI_2(s) + 2KNO_3$$

(Hint: Use NH_4OH for NH_3. See Question 2.)

_____

_____

_____

_____

_____

2. You may have noticed that some chemicals formed precipitates when mixed with ammonia, NH_3. This is because ammonia reacts with water to produce ammonium hydroxide, NH_4OH:

$$NH_3 + H_2O \rightarrow NH_4OH$$

To write the chemical equations for the precipitations with ammonia, you need to replace NH_3 with NH_4OH. For example,

$$Pb(NO_3)_2 + 2NH_4OH \rightarrow Pb(OH)_2(s) + 2NH_4NO_3$$

Write chemical equations for all the other precipitation reactions you observed with NH_3. In each case, replace NH_3 with NH_4OH.

_____

_____

_____

_____

3. Which reactions gave distinctive bubbles? What chemicals do all these reactions have in common? Write chemical equations to describe all the reactions that produced bubbles.

_____

_____

_____

4. Which reactions gave color changes but no precipitate?

_____

5. Which mixings could you have predicted in advance would not result in a reaction?

_____

NOW IT'S YOUR TURN!

1. Investigate further the reaction of $CuSO_4$ with NH_3. Try 1 drop of NH_3 with several drops of $CuSO_4$. Then try 1 drop of $CuSO_4$ with several drops of NH_3. What is distinctive about this reaction?

_____

_____

2. Investigate further the reaction of $AgNO_3$ with NH_3. Try 1 drop of NH_3 with several drops of $AgNO_3$. Then try 1 drop of $AgNO_3$ with several drops of NH_3. What's distinctive about this reaction?

_____

_____

3. Investigate further the reaction of $Pb(NO_3)_2$ with $NaOH$. Try 1 drop of $NaOH$ with several drops of $Pb(NO_3)_2$. Then try 1 drop of $Pb(NO_3)_2$ with several drops of $NaOH$. What's distinctive about this reaction?

_____

_____

4. A very distinctive precipitate is formed when H_2SO_4 and $CaCl_2$ are mixed. Repeat the reaction between sulfuric acid, H_2SO_4, and calcium chloride, $CaCl_2$. What is so distinctive about this precipitate?

_____

5. Challenge a friend. Hide the label and place 1 drop of either the top or bottom solution on your neighbor's grid (below). Ask him or her to identify it by using just 1 drop of any of the 13 chemicals. Repeat for each space.

$AgNO_3$	$CuSO_4$	Na_2CO_3	$FeCl_3$	$NaOH$	HCl	H_2SO_4	HNO_3
X	X	X	X	X	X	X	X
$Pb(NO_3)_2$	$CaCl_2$	Na_3PO_4	KI	NH_3	H_2SO_4	HNO_3	HCl

6. Ask a third person to line up 12 separate drops of any unknown chemical on your acetate. You go first. Add any chemical to the first drop and guess what the unknown is. The second player adds any chemical to the second drop and makes a guess. It's your turn again. Continue until there is a winner. Play this game several times until you can identify the unknown in just a few drops.

7. Choose a chemical and place 1 drop in each of the 11 spaces on a neighbor's grid (below). Challenge him or her to devise a way to uncover its identity in fewer drops than you used to identify his or her unknown.

1	2	3	4	5	6	7	8	9	10	11
X	X	X	X	X	X	X	X	X	X	X

20 IDENTIFICATION OF EIGHT UNKNOWN SOLUTIONS

Small-Scale Experiment for text section 15.2

OBJECTIVE

- **Identify** eight unknown solutions using known data and logical thinking.

INTRODUCTION

The art of logical thinking is essential to mastering chemistry. Although it is important to be familiar with many chemical facts so that you can utilize the language of chemistry effectively, it is even more important to be able to assimilate these facts and organize them in logical ways so they can be used to solve problems. The art of logical thinking is not difficult to acquire but it does require practice. Try out your own ability on the following logic problem.

During a chemistry class, five pairs of students are working on five different experiments at a row of lab stations numbered 1-5 consecutively. From the information given below, can you tell what each student's experiment is, at which lab station he or she is working, and who his or her lab partner is?

Clues:

1. The halogens experiment and all the other experiments are performed by lab partners of the opposite sex. For example, Ann Ion's lab partner is a boy.

2. Milli Liter and Ben Zene work together.

3. Charles Law does not work at lab station #2.

4. Molly Cool and her partner work between station #3 and the station occupied by Barry Um.

5. Phyllis Pipet, building a spectroscope, is not at #4.

6. Milli Liter does not work next to Molly Cool.

7. Earl N. Meyer works at #4.

8. Ionic reactions are being carried out at #5.

9. Hal Ogen is building a small-scale balance.

10. Only one of the Um twins, Francie or Barry, works at station #1 doing an acid-base titration.

Answers:

Lab Station	Boy	Girl	Experiment
1	Barry Um	Ann Ion	Acid-Base Titration
2	Hal Ogen	Molly Cool	Small-Scall Balance
3	Charles Law	Phyllis Pipet	Spectroscope
4	Earl N. Meyer	Francie Um	Halogens
5	Ben Zene	Milli Liter	Ionic Reactions

PURPOSE

In this lab you will mix eight unknown solutions two at a time just as you did in Small-Scale Experiment 19. The eight unknown solutions have been chosen at random from the original 13. You will compare your results with those you obtained in Small-Scale Experiment 19 and identify the eight unknown solutions through logical reasoning not unlike you used to solve the above problem. A successful conclusion to this lab does not require a Ph.D. in chemistry. It does require good organization, clear logical thinking, and good data.

SAFETY

- Wear your safety glasses.
- Use full small-scale pipets only for the carefully controlled delivery of liquids.

MATERIALS

Small-scale pipets of the following solutions:

ammonia (NH₃)	potassium iodide (KI)
sodium carbonate (Na₂CO₃)	calcium chloride (CaCl₂)
iron(III) chloride (FeCl₃)	

silver nitrate (AgNO₃)
sodium hydroxide (NaOH)
sodium phosphate (Na₃PO₄)
copper(II) sulfate (CuSO₄)
lead(II) nitrate (Pb(NO₃)₂)

hydrochloric acid (HCl)
sulfuric acid (H₂SO₄)
nitric acid (HNO₃)

Eight small-scale pipets of unknown solutions labeled with different numbers.

EQUIPMENT

small-scale reaction surface
empty pipet for stirring

EXPERIMENTAL PAGE

1. Obtain eight small-scale pipets labeled with numbers from your instructor. The eight pipets contain eight of the original 13 solutions from Small-Scale Experiment 19. Each is different. Write the numbers of the unknowns along the horizontal in Table 20.1 and in reverse order along the vertical. Mix 1 drop of each solution on the indicated X, just as you did in the last experiment. Stir each mixture by blowing air with an empty pipet. Record your results in Table 20.1.

Unknown numbers:

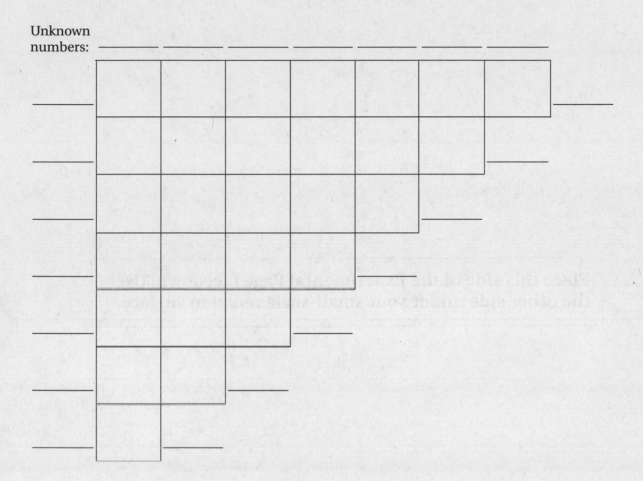

2. Compare your unknown reactions to those of the 13 solutions in Small-Scale Experiment 19, and see how many unknowns you can identify.

3. Devise a way to use the original 13 solutions to correctly identify your unknowns. To do this you should mix each unknown with several knowns, one at a time.

Place this side of the Experimental Page facedown. Use the other side under your small-scale reaction surface.

Name _____ Class _____ Date _____

EXPERIMENTAL DATA

Record you results in Tables 20.1 and 20.2 or tables like them in your notebook.

Table 20.1   Eight Unknowns

Unknown
numbers: _____ _____ _____ _____ _____ _____ _____

Table 20.2   Numbers, Formulas, and Names of Eight Unknown Solutions

Number							
Formula							
Name							

Name _____ Class _____ Date _____

CLEANING UP

Avoid contamination by cleaning up in a way that protects you and your environment. Carefully clean the small-scale reaction surface by absorbing the contents onto a paper towel. Rinse the reaction surface with a damp paper towel and dry it. Dispose of the paper towels in the waste bin. Wash your hands thoroughly with soap and water.

QUESTIONS FOR ANALYSIS

Use what you learned in this lab to answer the following questions.

1. What is the identity (name and formula) of each unknown you used in this lab?

   _____

2. Describe the logical thought process by which you arrived at your conclusions.

   _____

NOW IT'S YOUR TURN!

1. Obtain another set of eight unknown solutions. Devise a way to correctly identify your unknowns *without using known solutions*. (Hint: Design an 8 × 8 grid similar to the one on the Experimental Page. Mix the unknowns with each other two at a time.) Compare your unknown reactions to the data you collected from the 13 solutions in the last experiment. Remember, this time you may not use your known solutions to identify the unknowns. Report the results as you did before. Describe the logical thought process by which you arrived at your conclusions. Check your results with your instructor.

21 PAPER CHROMATOGRAPHY

Small-Scale Experiment for text section 16.3

OBJECTIVES

- **Separate** mixtures of compounds, using the technique of paper chromatography.
- **Identify** compounds contained in some common ink dyes.
- **Compare** formulations of inks in various brands of pens.

INTRODUCTION

Chromatography is a technique for separating mixtures of compounds. It is a powerful and versatile method used widely in chemistry and in the biological sciences. Chromatography can also be used to identify unknown substances. All of the several types of chromatography employ two different immiscible phases in contact with each other. One of the phases is moving, *the mobile phase*, and the other is not, *the stationary phase*. In paper chromatography, for example, a solvent moves from one end of a piece of paper to the other end, as the paper absorbs it. The solvent is the mobile phase because it is moving, and the paper is the stationary phase. (In reality, there are water molecules attached to the paper that serve as the stationary phase.)

A mixture of chemicals can be separated using paper chromatography. A small amount of mixture to be separated is placed near the edge of an absorbent paper. That edge of the paper is wetted with solvent. The solvent travels up the paper by capillary action, carrying the mixture with it. Separation occurs because different chemicals in the mixture travel different distances. The physical interaction of each compound in the mixture with the solvent (the mobile phase) and with the water molecules attached to the paper (the stationary phase) determines the distance it travels. Substances that dissolve more readily in the solvent will move farther than substances that have a higher affinity for the water attached to the paper. When the solvent has moved the entire length of the paper, the paper is removed from the solvent and dried. Once developed, the paper, called a *chromatogram*, will contain different chemicals located at different positions on the paper.

The various chemicals visible on the chromatogram can often be identified by their positions and/or their colors. If the mixture contains colored compounds, each different compound will appear on the chromatogram as a colored spot or a streak in a particular place. The color and location of each compound can be used as a basis for identification. The color and location of unknown compounds separated under specific chromatographic conditions can be matched with the color and location of known compounds subjected to the same conditions.

PURPOSE

In this lab you will use the technique of paper chromatography to separate the colored dyes in a variety of felt-tipped pens. You will then compare the chromatograms of the pens to those of known dyes to identify the dyes used in the pens.

SAFETY

- Wear your safety glasses.
- Assume that all the colored food and candy in this lab is contaminated with toxic chemicals. Do not eat or even taste anything in the laboratory.

MATERIALS

template cards	pencil
chromatography paper	stapler
typing paper	2 clear plastic cups
two sets of colored marking pens	solvent
scissors	1 set of FD&C dyes

EXPERIMENTAL PROCEDURE

1. Cut and mark two identical pieces of chromatography paper as follows. Use the cardboard template as a guide. Use *only black pencil* to write on the paper.

2. Obtain a set of marking pens and draw a small dot of ink from a red pen on the first pencil dot on one piece of chromatography paper. Continue placing colored dots on the pencil dots in the *same order as the visible spectrum*: red, orange, yellow, green, light blue, dark blue, and violet (ROY G BIV). Place other colors such as black, brown, and pink at the end. Record in your notebook the number, color, and brand of the pen.

3. Mark the second piece of chromatography paper with a second set of marker pens (a different brand). Place the colors *in the same order* as on your first chromatogram. Record this data in your notebook.

4. Staple the two papers into cylinders, dot side out, being careful not to allow the edges to touch one another (Figure 21.1).

Figure 21.1

Figure 21.2

5. Wet the bottom of two plastic cups with solvent and place a paper cylinder in each, colored sides down. Initially, the colored dots should be above the solvent as shown in Figure 21.2.

6. Spot the following FD&C dyes onto a third chromatography paper: red #3, red #40, yellow #5, yellow #6, green #3, blue #1, and blue #2. These dyes will help you to identify the dyes in the marking pens. Use a tiny triangle of *typing paper* to spot these dyes onto the chromatography paper. Cut the triangle and wet one tip in a dye solution. Touch the wet tip lightly to a pencil spot. Use a new triangle for each different dye.

7. While you wait for the solvent to move up the paper or elute (about 10–15 minutes), begin answering the Questions for Analysis.

8. Remove the paper cylinders when the solvent reaches $\frac{1}{2}-1$ cm from the top of the chromatography paper. Mark the highest point the solvent reached with a pencil and allow the paper to dry upright on a paper towel. When the paper is dry, remove the staples. Keep all of the chromatograms obtained from this experiment and attach them to your laboratory notebook or report.

EXPERIMENTAL DATA

Tape or staple your dry chromatograms here or in your lab notebook for easy reference.

CLEANING UP

Avoid contamination by cleaning up in a way that protects you and your environment. Leave your chromatograms to dry in a place designated by your instructor. Once dry, attach each to your laboratory notebook or report. Dispose of extra solvents down the drain, and rinse and dry the plastic cups. Clean up the area thoroughly, and be sure to recycle usable pieces of paper. Wash your hands thoroughly with soap and water.

QUESTIONS FOR ANALYSIS

Use what you learned in this lab to answer the following questions.

1. What happens to the ink spots as the chromatogram develops? Why?

_____

2. If one dye moves faster than another, which one dissolves more readily in the moving solvent? Which one dissolves more readily in the water that is attached to the stationary paper?

_____

_____

Name _____ Class _____ Date _____

3. Which ink dyes (specify original color) are probably made up of only one compound? How can you tell?

_____

4. How can you tell which ink dyes are made up of two compounds?

_____

5. Which ink dyes are made up of more than two compounds?

_____

6. How can you tell if both brands of pens use the same combination of dyes to make black? Brown? How can you tell?

_____

7. Compare your two chromatograms of the pens by placing one directly above the other. Which colors of ink use the same compound(s) for both brands?

_____

8. Compare your two chromatograms by placing them side by side. By noting the color and position of each spot, tell which pens (color and brand) contain the same (a) light blue dye; (b) red dye; (c) yellow dye.

_____

9. You can identify the ink dyes by their *positions* and *colors* on the chromatogram. Compare the positions and colors of the known FD&C dyes with the positions and colors of the unknown dyes in the pens. Identify as many dyes as you can like this: "The orange brand X pen contains red #40 and yellow #5."

_____

_____

10. Which ink dyes (state the brand name and color) can you *not* identify?

_____

NOW IT'S YOUR TURN!

1. Design and carry out some experiments to answer one or more of the following questions:

a. What are the identities of the dyes in other brands of pens? How do they compare to the ones you already tested?

_____

b. What is the effect of the kind of paper you used on your results?

_____

_____

Name _____ Class _____ Date _____

    c. What is the effect of the solvent you use?

_____

2. Use paper chromatography to identify dyes in various consumer food products like soda pop, powdered drinks, instant breakfast drinks, gelatin, candy, and food coloring. You may have to invent ways to extract the dyes from the products.

_____

_____

3. In chromatography, the symbol R_f is used to denote the position of a component on a chromatogram relative to the distance the solvent moved. This R_f value is a quantitative reflection of the physical interaction of each component with the mobile phase (the solvent) and stationary phase (the water molecules on the paper).

$$R_f = \frac{\text{distance component moved}}{\text{distance solvent moved}}$$

Measure the distance from the origin to the center of each spot and the distance from the origin to the solvent front. Calculate the R_f values for each spot. The best way to estimate the center of a noncircular spot is to draw the best ellipse around the spot and estimate its center.

4. Water is a very polar solvent that has a particularly strong tendency to form hydrogen bonds. Isopropyl alcohol (rubbing alcohol) is less polar than water and hydrogen bonds less strongly. Because of their differences in polarity and hydrogen bonding, these solvents will interact differently in the chromatographic separation of mixtures.

    Generally, if the solvent (mobile phase) is more polar than the stationary phase, the more polar compounds will tend to dissolve more readily and spend more time in the solvent. As a result, they will move farther than the less polar ones. The more polar compounds will appear near the top of the chromatogram, and the less polar compounds will appear near the bottom.

    If the solvent (mobile phase) is less polar than the stationary phase, the more polar compounds will spend more time in the stationary phase. As a result, they will move more slowly and appear near the bottom of the chromatogram.

    What will happen if you run two chromatograms of pen dyes, one in a very polar solvent like 0.1% aqueous NaCl, and one in a less polar solvent like 70% rubbing alcohol? Try it to see for yourself! Particularly, note any differences in the two chromatograms. Explain the differences.

22 ELECTROLYTES

OBJECTIVES

- **Observe** and **record** the electrical conductivity of water solutions and solid compounds.
- **Classify** substances as strong electrolytes, weak electrolytes, or nonelectrolytes using conductivity data.
- **Observe** the phenomena of *deliquescence* and *water of hydration*.

INTRODUCTION

Electrolytes are compounds that exist as dissolved ions in water solutions. A distinguishing macroscopic property of electrolyte solutions is that they conduct electricity. Molten electrolytes also conduct electricity. The submicroscopic interpretation is that the ions are free to move about in the liquid, and these charged particles carry the electrical current.

PURPOSE

In this experiment you will investigate water solutions of chemicals by testing them for conductivity. You will then evaporate the water and test them again. You will interpret your results in terms of the submicroscopic behavior of atoms and molecules. Finally, you will test various solutions to determine their relative tendencies to conduct electricity, and again interpret your results in terms of atoms and molecules. You will classify solutions as *strong electrolytes*, those that readily conduct electricity; *weak electrolytes*, those that conduct electricity only weakly; and *nonelectrolytes*, those that do not conduct electricity.

The small-scale conductivity apparatus is shown in Figure 22.1. When the two leads are immersed in a drop of solution or in a solid that conducts electricity, the light emitting diode (LED) will glow.

drop of CaCl$_2$ (aq)   LED

perf board

battery snap

9 volt

resistor
330 Ω (ohms)

Figure 22.1 *Conductivity apparatus*

SAFETY

- Wear your safety glasses.
- Use full small-scale pipets only for the carefully controlled delivery of liquids.

MATERIALS

Small-scale pipets of the following solutions:

calcium chloride ($CaCl_2$)
sodium hydrogen sulfate ($NaHSO_4$)
sodium phosphate (Na_3PO_4)
sodium hydrogen carbonate ($NaHCO_3$)
water (H_2O)
2-propanol ($CH_3CHOHCH_3$)
hydrogen peroxide (H_2O_2)

iron(III) chloride ($FeCl_3$)
aluminum chloride ($AlCl_3$)
zinc chloride ($ZnCl_2$)
sodium carbonate (Na_2CO_3)
ethanol (CH_3CH_2OH)
methanol (CH_3OH)

copper(II) sulfate ($CuSO_4$)
sodium hydroxide (NaOH)

Solids:

sodium chloride (NaCl)
potassium iodide (KI)
sodium carbonate (Na_2CO_3)

potassium chloride (KCl)
calcium chloride ($CaCl_2$)
sucrose ($C_{12}H_{22}O_{11}$)

EQUIPMENT

small-scale reaction surface
conductivity apparatus
glass slide
hot plate

EXPERIMENTAL PAGE

Part A. Conductivity of Ionic Compounds

1. Place 1 drop of each indicated chemical solution on a glass slide in the following arrangement, and test each drop for conductivity with the conductivity apparatus. Be sure to *clean and dry* the conductivity leads after each test.

$CaCl_2$	$NaHSO_4$	$NaOH$	Na_3PO_4	$NaHCO_3$
x	x	x	x	x
x	x	x	x	x
$FeCl_3$	$CuSO_4$	$AlCl_3$	$ZnCl_2$	Na_2CO_3

2. Now evaporate water from the droplets by putting the glass slide on a hot plate. Test for conductivity again. **Caution:** *The glass will be hot. Handle with tongs or a plastic spatula.*

3. Allow the slide to cool and observe any changes over time. Meanwhile, go on to Part B.

Part B. Conductivity of Solids

4. Place 1 grain of each solid (*s*) in the indicated place and test each for conductivity. Then add 1 drop of water to each and test the "wet" mixture for conductivity.

$NaCl(s)$	$KCl(s)$	$KI(s)$	$CaCl_2(s)$	$Na_2CO_3(s)$	$C_{12}H_{22}O_{11}(s)$
salt	"lite" salt	in iodized salt	ice-melter	washing soda	table sugar

Part C. Conductivity of Liquids

5. Place 1 drop of each liquid (*l*) in the indicated place and test each for conductivity. Then add 1 drop of water and test the "wet" mixture for conductivity.

$H_2O(l)$	$CH_3CH_2OH(l)$	$CH_3CHOHCH_3(l)$	$CH_3OH(l)$	$H_2O_2(l)$
water	ethanol grain alcohol	2-propanol rubbing alcohol	methanol wood alcohol	hydrogen peroxide a disinfectant

Place this side of the Experimental Page facedown. Use the other side under your small-scale reaction surface.

Name _____ Class _____ Date _____

EXPERIMENTAL DATA

Record your results in Tables 22.1, 22.2, and 22.3. or tables like them in your notebook.

Table 22.1 Conductivity of Ionic Compounds

Compound	Conducts in Solution?	Conducts when Evaporated?	Compound	Conducts in Solution?	Conducts when Evaporated?
$CaCl_2$			$FeCl_3$		
$NaHSO_4$			$CuSO_4$		
$NaOH$			$AlCl_3$		
Na_3PO_4			$ZnCl_2$		
$NaHCO_3$			Na_2CO_3		

Which of the above solutions seems to be sluggish to evaporate or became wet upon standing in air?

Table 22.2 Conductivity of Dry and Wet Solids

	$NaCl(s)$	$KCl(s)$	$KI(s)$	$CaCl_2(s)$	$Na_2CO_3(s)$	$C_{12}H_{22}O_{11}(s)$
Conducts: Dry?						
Wet?						

Table 22.3 Conductivity of Dry and Wet Liquids

	$H_2O(l)$	$CH_3CH_2OH(l)$	$CH_3CHOHCH_3(l)$	$CH_3OH(l)$	$H_2O_2(l)$
Conducts: Dry?					
Wet?					

Prentice Hall, Inc. All rights reserved.

Electrolytes   **161**

Name _____ Class _____ Date _____

CLEANING UP

Avoid contamination by cleaning up in a way that protects you and your environment. Carefully clean the small-scale reaction surface by absorbing the contents onto a paper towel. Rinse the reaction surface with a damp paper towel and dry it. Dispose of the paper towels in the waste bin. Clean the glass slide by rinsing it with water and drying it with a paper towel. Wash your hands thoroughly with soap and water.

QUESTIONS FOR ANALYSIS

Use what you learned in this lab to answer the following questions.

1. **a.** Do any of the solids in any part of this experiment conduct electricity?
    b. What must be added before a solid will conduct electricity?
    c. Does this work every time? Give an example.

    _____

    _____

2. A substance exhibits *deliquescence* when it absorbs enough water from the air to completely dissolve. Which solutions in Part A are deliquescent? (Hint: They seemed sluggish to evaporate or became wet upon standing in air.)

    _____

3. Water molecules that are fixed in the lattice of an ionic compound when in the solid form make up the *water of hydration*. Water of hydration will evaporate by strong heating often with a dramatic change in color. Which solids in Part A, Step 2, contain water of hydration?

    _____

4. You can picture solid sodium chloride as a regular ordered arrangement of atoms called an ionic lattice (Figure 22.2). Solid KCl and KI are similar to NaCl. Draw them and explain the result of the conductivity test in terms of your drawing.

Figure 22.2 *Ionic lattice of NaCl*

_____

_____

5. You know that solutions that conduct electricity do so because they contain ions that are free to move about in solution. For example, a solution of aqueous sodium chloride can be pictured as in Figure 22.3. Draw pictures to represent the solutions of KI and KCl. Explain the conductivity test in terms of your pictures.

Figure 22.3 *Drop of aqueous NaCl*

_____

_____

6. Which of the liquids in Part C conduct electricity? Which conduct electricity when water is added?

_____

7. **a.** Make a list of electrolytes and another list of nonelectrolytes.

b. Pure water is a nonelectrolyte. Predict what will happen if you test tap water for conductivity.

_____

_____

8. Study the chemical formulas of the electrolytes and nonelectrolytes. What chemical species do all electrolytes contain? How are the nonelectrolytes different? Draw a conclusion based on your answers to these questions.

_____

_____

9. You know that when an ionic solid dissolves in water, water molecules attract the ions causing them to come apart or dissociate. The resulting dissolved ions are electrically charged particles that allow the solution to conduct electricity. A chemical equation that represents this phenomenon is written like this:

$$NaCl(s) \rightarrow Na^+(aq) + Cl^-(aq) \text{ or } CaCl_2(s) \rightarrow Ca^{2+}(aq) + 2Cl^-(aq)$$

Write a similar chemical equation for each electrolyte you observed in this lab to show how the ions come apart in water.

_____

_____

_____

_____

_____

NOW IT'S YOUR TURN!

1. Using a soda straw, obtain small samples of these household products: a solid toilet-bowl cleaner, a small piece of seltzer tablet, a baking powder (not soda!). Add a drop of water to each. Test for conductivity. Explain why these substances do not react until water is added.

_____

_____

2. Test these aqueous solutions for conductivity:

1 drop each:	1 drop each:	1 drop each:	1 drop each:

Solutions that cause the LED to glow brightly are called *strong electrolytes*. Those that make it glow less brightly are called *weak electrolytes*. Make a list of the strong and weak electrolytes, and propose an explanation for the difference in the brightness of the LED.

_____

_____

_____

23 SOLUBILITY RULES

Small-Scale Experiment for text section 18.1

OBJECTIVES

- **Observe** and **record** chemical changes that form precipitates.
- **Derive** general solubility rules from experimental data.
- **Describe** precipitation reactions by writing net ionic equations.

INTRODUCTION

In the study of chemical reactions it is helpful to have an idea of which compounds can be expected to form precipitates. A *soluble* compound will dissolve readily in water and, therefore, will *not* form a precipitate. An *insoluble* compound will not dissolve readily in water and, therefore, *will* form a precipitate.

How do we know which ionic compounds form precipitates and which do not? We can make a large number of mixings involving many different cations and anions. By observing the results and correlating them in a logical fashion, we can formulate some general solubility rules based on the formation of precipitates.

These guidelines can be used to describe the behavior of ionic compounds in solution and to determine which compounds form precipitates. For example, if a sodium ion is used as a probe and a large number of observations indicate that no precipitates containing the sodium ion are formed in aqueous solution, one conclusion might be: "All sodium salts are soluble in water. They do not form precipitates." In fact, a large number of such observations have been made, and it is well known that all sodium salts are water-soluble and that there are no common exceptions to this rule.

PURPOSE

In this lab you will carry out an experiment from whose data you can derive some general solubility guidelines or rules. You will do this by mixing a number of cation solutions and anion solutions two by two. Each anion solution will be used as a probe to determine which cations form precipitates with that anion.

Careful selection of compounds to represent cations and anions is important. For example, the solutions to represent anions are chosen to be compounds of sodium because we know that all sodium compounds are soluble in water, so any precipitate we see will be typical of the anion. Sodium ion, Na^+, will always be a "spectator ion" and will not take part in any chemical reaction.

Keep in mind that you need not perform mixings between solutions having a common ion. For example, it should be obvious that $CuSO_4$ will not react with Na_2SO_4 because both compounds contain the sulfate ion. Thus, with a little planning you can avoid any unnecessary mixings.

- Wear your safety glasses.
- Use full small-scale pipets only for the carefully controlled delivery of liquids.

MATERIALS

Small-scale pipets containing solutions representing cations:

aluminum chloride ($AlCl_3$)   ammonium chloride (NH_4Cl)
sodium chloride (NaCl)   magnesium sulfate ($MgSO_4$)
calcium chloride ($CaCl_2$)   zinc chloride ($ZnCl_2$)
potassium iodide (KI)   iron(III) chloride ($FeCl_3$)

lead(II) nitrate ($Pb(NO_3)_2$)
silver nitrate ($AgNO_3$)
copper(II) sulfate ($CuSO_4$)

Small-scale pipets containing solutions representing anions:

sodium carbonate (Na_2CO_3)   sodium hydroxide (NaOH)
sodium phosphate (Na_3PO_4)   sodium chloride (NaCl)
sodium nitrate ($NaNO_3$)   sodium sulfate (Na_2SO_4)

EQUIPMENT

small-scale reaction surface
empty pipet for stirring

EXPERIMENTAL PAGE

Mix 1 drop of each. Stir by gently blowing air through a clean, dry pipet.

Cations \ Anions	Na_2CO_3 (CO_3^{2-})	NaCl (Cl^-)	NaOH (OH^-)	$NaNO_3$ (NO_3^-)	Na_3PO_4 (PO_4^{3-})	Na_2SO_4 (SO_4^{2-})
$AlCl_3$ (Al^{3+})	X	X	X	X	X	X
NH_4Cl (NH_4^+)	X	X	X	X	X	X
$CaCl_2$ (Ca^{2+})	X	X	X	X	X	X
$CuSO_4$ (Cu^{2+})	X	X	X	X	X	X
NaCl (Na^+)	X	X	X	X	X	X
$FeCl_3$ (Fe^{3+})	X	X	X	X	X	X
$Pb(NO_3)_2$ (Pb^{2+})	X	X	X	X	X	X
$MgSO_4$ (Mg^{2+})	X	X	X	X	X	X
KI (K^+)	X	X	X	X	X	X
$AgNO_3$ (Ag^+)	X	X	X	X	X	X
$ZnCl_2$ (Zn^{2+})	X	X	X	X	X	X

Place this side of the Experimental Page facedown. Use the other side under your small-scale reaction surface.

Name _____ Class _____ Date _____

EXPERIMENTAL DATA

Record your results in Table 23.1 or a table like it in your notebook.

Table 23.1   Anion-Cation Mixings

Anions Cations	Na_2CO_3 (CO_3^{2-})	NaCl (Cl^-)	NaOH (OH^-)	$NaNO_3$ (NO_3^-)	Na_3PO_4 (PO_4^{3-})	Na_2SO_4 (SO_4^{2-})
$AlCl_3$ (Al^{3+})						
NH_4Cl (NH_4^+)						
$CaCl_2$ (Ca^{2+})						
$CuSO_4$ (Cu^{2+})						
NaCl (Na^+)						
$FeCl_3$ (Fe^{3+})						
$Pb(NO_3)_2$ (Pb^{2+})						
$MgSO_4$ (Mg^{2+})						
KI (K^+)						
$AgNO_3$ (Ag^+)						
$ZnCl_2$ (Zn^{2-})						

CLEANING UP

Avoid contamination by cleaning up in a way that protects you and your environment. Carefully clean the small-scale reaction surface by absorbing the contents onto a paper towel. Rinse the reaction surface with a damp paper towel and dry it. Dispose of the paper towels in the waste bin. Wash your hands thoroughly with soap and water.

Name _____ Class _____ Date _____

QUESTIONS FOR ANALYSIS

Use what you learned in this lab to answer the following questions.

1. Examine your data for each column of anions. Which anions generally form precipitates? What are the exceptions? Which anions generally do not form precipitates? What are the exceptions?

   _____

   _____

   _____

2. Examine your data for each row of cations. Which cations generally do not form precipitates?

   _____

3. You have seen that precipitation reactions can be written as double-replacement reactions in which the ions of the reactants switch partners to form products. For example, aluminum chloride reacts with sodium hydroxide to form a precipitate of aluminum hydroxide and sodium chloride:

$$AlCl_3 + 3NaOH \rightarrow Al(OH)_3(s) + 3NaCl$$

Write and balance complete chemical equations for the other precipitation reactions you observed for aluminum chloride and those you observed for copper sulfate.

   _____

   _____

   _____

   _____

   _____

4. You have seen that ionic compounds are electrolytes in water solution. The reason is that their ionic lattices break apart in water, and the freed ions carry the electric current. For example, $AlCl_3$ exists in water solution as Al^{3+} and Cl^- ions. Similarly, sodium hydroxide exists in water as Na^+ and OH^- ions. Therefore, when aqueous aluminum chloride and aqueous sodium hydroxide react, the reactants are really these ions: Al^{3+}, Cl^-, Na^+, and OH^-. The sodium chloride product also exists as ions because it does not precipitate. The ionic equation for the reaction between aluminum chloride and sodium hydroxide is written like this:

$$Al^{3+} + 3Cl^- + 3Na^+ + 3OH^- \rightarrow Al(OH)_3(s) + 3Na^+ + 3Cl^-$$

The net ionic equation is obtained by eliminating the ions common to both sides of the equation:

$$Al^{3+} + 3OH^- \rightarrow Al(OH)_3(s)$$

Write net ionic equations to describe all the reactions you observed that formed precipitates. You may begin by identifying the precipitate and working backwards. The net ionic equations for the three precipitation reactions involving the aluminum ion are written like this:

$$2Al^{3+} + 3CO_3^{2-} \rightarrow Al_2(CO_3)_3(s) \text{ (white)}$$

$$Al^{3+} + 3OH^- \rightarrow Al(OH)_3(s) \text{ (white)}$$

$$Al^{3+} + PO_4^{3-} \rightarrow AlPO_4(s) \text{ (white)}$$

_____

_____

_____

_____

_____

_____

_____

_____

_____

_____

NOW IT'S YOUR TURN!

1. Repeat the reaction between silver nitrate, $AgNO_3$, and sodium hydroxide, NaOH. This mixture produces water, sodium nitrate, and silver oxide rather than silver hydroxide. Write and balance a chemical equation to describe this reaction. What is the distinctive color of silver oxide?

_____

2. Repeat the reaction between calcium chloride, $CaCl_2$, and sodium sulfate, Na_2SO_4. Write and balance a chemical equation to describe this reaction. What is distinctive about this reaction?

_____

3. Repeat the reaction between aluminum chloride, $AlCl_3$, and sodium hydroxide, NaOH. Write and balance a chemical equation to describe this reaction. Now add several more drops of NaOH. What is distinctive about this reaction?

_____

4. Repeat the reaction between zinc chloride, $ZnCl_2$, and sodium hydroxide, NaOH. Write and balance a chemical equation to describe this reaction. Now add several more drops of NaOH. What is distinctive about this reaction?

_____

_____

5. Repeat the reaction between lead(II) nitrate, $Pb(NO_3)_2$, and sodium hydroxide, NaOH. Write and balance a chemical equation to describe this reaction. Now add several more drops of NaOH. What is distinctive about this reaction?

_____

_____

24 FACTORS AFFECTING THE RATE OF A CHEMICAL REACTION

Small-Scale Experiment for text section 19.1

OBJECTIVES

- **Define** rate of reaction in terms of bubble formation.
- **Observe** and **record** the effect of temperature, concentration, and surface area on rate of reaction.

INTRODUCTION

You know that energy is required to cook food. The energy may come from boiling water or from the heating elements of a microwave or a conventional oven. Whatever the case, the warmer the temperature, the faster food cooks. On the other hand, in order to preserve food, it's common to place it in a refrigerator or a freezer. The cool temperature in the refrigerator helps to retard spoiling. The warmer the temperature, the faster food spoils. Temperature has an effect on the rate at which food cooks and also on the rate at which it spoils. When food is cooked or when it spoils, many chemical reactions take place. But temperature is just one factor that affects the speed at which chemical reactions occur.

If you've ever started a camp fire, you know that small wood shavings are more easily lit than large logs. Given equal volumes of wood in the forms of shavings and a single log, the wood shavings have more exposed surface area than does the log. The wood in the form of shavings makes more surfaces available for ignition. The burning of wood involves several chemical reactions. Increased surface area has an effect on how fast a given chemical reaction occurs.

Fire is a rapid reaction of a fuel with oxygen that gives off a lot of heat. The more oxygen there is available to the reaction, the faster the reaction will go. That is, the greater the concentration of oxygen, the faster the reaction will go. A camp fire burns at a certain rate in air where the concentration of oxygen is only about 20% by volume. If that concentration is cut down by the smothering effect of a fire extinguisher, the fire dies down or goes out; the reaction slows or stops. Thus concentration affects reaction rate.

PURPOSE

In this lab you will explore these and other factors that affect the rates of chemical reactions. You will examine reactions of hydrochloric acid with magnesium metal, with solid calcium carbonate, and with aqueous sodium hydrogen carbonate. Careful observations will enable you to derive a working definition of *rate of reaction* in terms of the products evolved. You will then examine how temperature, surface area, and concentration affect rate of reaction.

SAFETY

- Wear your safety glasses.
- Use full small-scale pipets only for the carefully controlled delivery of liquids.

MATERIALS

Small-scale pipets of the following solutions:

hydrochloric acid (HCl)

sodium hydrogen carbonate (NaHCO$_3$)
Solids:
magnesium (Mg)
calcium carbonate(CaCO$_3$)

EQUIPMENT

small-scale reaction surface
ice
hot water
two plastic cups

EXPERIMENTAL PAGE

1. What is rate of reaction? Make the following mixings and record your results in Table 24.1

	1 piece Mg	1 piece $CaCO_3$	1 drop $NaHCO_3$
6 drops HCl			

2. What is the effect of temperature on rate of reaction? Cool one HCl pipet in ice water; warm another in hot water from the tap; and mix the following, one pair at a time. Record your results in Table 24.2.

	1 piece Mg	1 piece $CaCO_3$	1 drop $NaHCO_3$
6 drops cold HCl			
6 drops warm HCl			

3. What is the effect of surface area of Mg or $CaCO_3$ on rate of reaction? Choose two equal-size pieces of Mg, and break or cut one. Repeat for $CaCO_3$. Make the following mixings and record your results in Table 24.3.

	1 piece Mg	Cut or crushed Mg	1 piece $CaCO_3$	Crushed $CaCO_3$
6 drops HCl				

4. What is the effect of concentration of HCl on rate of reaction? Make the following mixings and record your results in Table 24.4.

	1 piece Mg	1 piece $CaCO_3$	1 drop $NaHCO_3$
10 drops HCl			
5 drops HCl + 5 drops H_2O			
1 drop HCl + 9 drops H_2O			

Place this side of the Experimental Page facedown. Use
the other side under your small-scale reaction surface.

Name _____ Class _____ Date _____

EXPERIMENTAL DATA

Record your results in Tables 24.1, 24.2, 24.3, and 24.4 or tables like them in your notebook.

Table 24.1   Exploring Rate of Reaction

	1 piece Mg	1 piece $CaCO_3$	1 drop $NaHCO_3$
6 drops HCl			

Table 24.2   Effect of Temperature

	1 piece Mg	1 piece $CaCO_3$	1 drop $NaHCO_3$
6 drops cold HCl			
6 drops warm HCl			

Table 24.3   Effect of Surface Area

	1 piece Mg	Cut or crushed Mg	1 piece $CaCO_3$	Crushed $CaCO_3$
6 drops HCl				

Table 24.4   Effect of Concentration

	1 piece Mg	1 piece $CaCO_3$	1 drop $NaHCO_3$
10 drops HCl			
5 drops HCl + 5 drops H_2O			
1 drop HCl + 9 drops H_2O			

Name _____ Class _____ Date _____

CLEANING UP

Avoid contamination by cleaning up in a way that protects you and your environment. Carefully isolate any unreacted solids and place them in the proper recycling container. Clean the small-scale reaction surface by absorbing the contents onto a paper towel. Rinse the reaction surface with a damp paper towel and dry it. Dispose of the paper towels in the waste bin. Wash your hands thoroughly with soap and water.

QUESTIONS FOR ANALYSIS

Use what you learned in this lab to answer the following questions.

1. Define rate of reaction in terms of bubble formation. How does rate of reaction change with time?

   _____

2. What is the effect of temperature on rate of reaction?

   _____

3. What is the effect of the surface area of Mg or $CaCO_3$ on rate of reaction?

   _____

4. What is the effect of concentration of HCl on rate of reaction?

   _____

5. Magnesium reacts with acid to yield hydrogen gas and a salt. Write the balanced chemical equation for the reaction of hydrochloric acid with magnesium.

   _____

6. Recall that an acid reacts with a carbonate or hydrogen carbonate to yield carbon dioxide gas, water, and a salt. Write the balanced chemical equations for the reactions of hydrochloric acid with calcium carbonate and with sodium hydrogen carbonate.

   _____

   _____

NOW IT'S YOUR TURN!

1. Carry out the following reactions. What happens in each case? Write chemical equations to describe each reaction.

   a. $Pb(NO_3)_2 + KI \rightarrow$ _____

   _____

   b. $H_2SO_4 + CaCl_2 \rightarrow$ _____

   _____

25 LE CHÂTELIER'S PRINCIPLE AND CHEMICAL EQUILIBRIUM

Small-Scale Experiment for text section 19.2

OBJECTIVES

- **Observe** and **record** how a chemical system at equilibrium responds to changes in concentration of reactants or products.
- **Describe** shifts in equilibrium in terms of Le Châtelier's principle.

INTRODUCTION

If you've ever watched a game of football, you know that it has become very specialized. Coaches design special offenses and defenses for various down and distance situations, as well as for positions of the ball on the field, the score, and the time remaining in the game. For example, offensive and defensive strategies are quite different for a third down and one situation than for a first down and ten. As a result, several offensive and defensive players often run on and off the field after each play. One thing remains constant: there are only eleven players per team on the field for any given play. This is an example of a dynamic equilibrium. A dynamic equilibrium is one in which forward reactions (players running on the field) take place at the same rate as reverse reactions (players running off the field). There is no net change in the number of players on the field.

You learned in Section 19.1 that chemical systems often reach a state of dynamic equilibrium. In a system at chemical equilibrium, the rate of the forward reaction equals the rate of the reverse reaction. By adding or taking away reactants and/or products, we can change the balance of reactants and products. The position of the equilibrium is governed by Le Châtelier's principle.

Le Châtelier's principle says that if a system at equilibrium is stressed, the equilibrium balance will shift in a direction that will relieve the stress. For example, if we add a reactant, the equilibrium will shift toward products (to the right) so that there is a different balance of reactants and products. Similarly, if we add products, it will shift toward reactants (to the left).

PURPOSE

In this lab you will investigate chemical systems at equilibrium. You will disturb them by adding or subtracting reactants or products and observe how the equilibrium system responds. You will attempt to explain those changes in terms of Le Châtelier's principle.

SAFETY 🥽

- Wear your safety glasses.
- Use full small-scale pipets only for the carefully controlled delivery of liquids.

MATERIALS

Small-scale pipets of the following solutions:

sodium carbonate (Na₂CO₃)   bromthymol blue (BTB)
ammonia (NH₃)   sodium phosphate (Na₃PO₄)
potassium iodide (KI)   sodium thiosulfate (Na₂S₂O₃)

hydrochloric acid (HCl)
nitric acid (HNO₃)

sodium hydroxide (NaOH)
lead(II) nitrate (Pb(NO₃)₂)
copper(II) sulfate (CuSO₄)
silver nitrate (AgNO₃)

EQUIPMENT

small-scale reaction surface
empty pipet for stirring
plastic cup

EXPERIMENTAL PAGE

Mix the following. Stir each mixture thoroughly by blowing air through a pipet. The chemical equations describe the changes you observe.

1. Mix 1 drop BTB and 1 drop HCl (H⁺). Record your observations in Table 25.1. Now add just enough NaOH to induce another change. Alternately add more HCl and NaOH.

$$HBTB \rightleftharpoons H^+ + BTB^-$$
   yellow   blue

2. Mix 1 drop BTB and 1 drop NH_3. Record your observations in Table 25.1. Now add just enough HCl (H⁺) to effect a change.

$$NH_3 + HOH \rightleftharpoons NH_4^+ + OH^- \qquad NH_3 + H^+ \rightleftharpoons NH_4^+$$

3. Mix 1 drop NH_3 and 2 drops $CuSO_4$ (Cu^{2+}). Record your observations in Table 25.1. Now add, with stirring, just enough NH_3 to effect a change. Add HCl, with stirring, until the light blue precipitate returns. Add more HCl until the precipitate disappears. Repeat all this until you are sure of what you see.

$$Cu^{2+} + 2OH^- \rightleftharpoons Cu(OH)_2(s) \text{ (light blue precipitate)}$$
$$Cu^{2+} + 4NH_3 \rightleftharpoons Cu(NH_3)_4^{2+} \text{ (royal blue solution)}$$
$$H^+ + OH^- \rightleftharpoons HOH$$

4. Mix 1 drop $Pb(NO_3)_2$ (Pb^{2+}) and 1 drop KI (I⁻). Record your observations in Table 25.1. Now add, with stirring, enough NaOH to effect a change. Now add HNO_3.

$$Pb^{2+} + 2I^- \rightleftharpoons PbI_2(s) \text{ (bright yellow precipitate)}$$
$$Pb^{2+} + 2OH^- \rightleftharpoons Pb(OH)_2(s) \text{ (milky white precipitate)}$$

5. Mix 1 drop $Pb(NO_3)_2$ and 1 drop NaOH with stirring. Record your observations in Table 25.1. Now add more NaOH, drop by drop with stirring, until a change occurs. Finally add nitric acid, HNO_3 (H⁺), drop by drop, slowly, with stirring, until the first change occurs.

$$Pb^{2+} + 2OH^- \rightleftharpoons Pb(OH)_2(s) \qquad Pb^{2+} + 3OH^- \rightleftharpoons Pb(OH)_3^-$$
$$H^+ + OH^- \rightleftharpoons HOH$$

6. Add 2 drops $AgNO_3$ to a plastic cup. Now add one drop of each of the chemicals in the left column, one at a time. Stir and observe after each addition. When a change occurs, record your observations in Table 25.1. Go on to the next chemical. Near the last addition, you may need to add a few more drops of $AgNO_3$.

Add these chemicals in this order

a. 1 drop Na_2CO_3
b. HNO_3
c. NaOH
d. HCl

e. NH_3
f. KI
g. $Na_2S_2O_3$
h. Na_3PO_4

Equations that account for changes

a. $2Ag^+ + CO_3^{2-} \rightleftharpoons Ag_2CO_3(s)$
b. $CO_3^{2-} + 2H^+ \rightleftharpoons HOH + CO_2(g)$
c. $2Ag^+ + 2OH^- \rightleftharpoons Ag_2O(s) + H_2O$
d. $H^+ + OH^- \rightleftharpoons HOH$
   $Ag^+ + Cl^- \rightleftharpoons AgCl$
e. $Ag^+ + 2NH_3 \rightleftharpoons Ag(NH_3)_2^+$
f. $Ag^+ + I^- \rightleftharpoons AgI(s)$
g. $Ag^+ + S_2O_3^{2-} \rightleftharpoons AgS_2O_3^-$
h. $3Ag^+ + PO_4^{3-} \rightleftharpoons Ag_3PO_4(s)$

Place this side of the Experimental Page facedown. Use the other side under your small-scale reaction surface.

Name _____ Class _____ Date _____

EXPERIMENTAL DATA

Record your results in Table 25.1 or a table like it in your notebook.

Table 25.1 Dynamic Equilibria

1. BTB + HCl _____

    + NaOH _____

    _____

2. BTB + NH_3 _____

    + HCl: _____

3. NH_3 + $CuSO_4$ _____

    More NH_3 _____

    + HCl _____

    More HCl _____

4. $Pb(NO_3)_2$ + KI _____

    + NaOH: _____

    + HNO_3 _____

5. $Pb(NO_3)_2$ + NaOH _____

    More NaOH _____

    + HNO_3 _____

6. $AgNO_3$ + Na_2CO_3 _____

    + HNO_3 _____

    + NaOH _____

    + HCl _____

    + NH_3 _____

    + KI _____

    + $Na_2S_2O_3$ _____

    + Na_3PO_4 _____

CLEANING UP

Avoid contamination by cleaning up in a way that protects you and your environment. Carefully clean the small-scale reaction surface by absorbing the contents onto a paper towel. Rinse the reaction surface with a damp paper towel and dry it. Dispose of the paper towels in the waste bin. Wash your hands thoroughly with soap and water.

Name _____ Class _____ Date _____

QUESTIONS FOR ANALYSIS

Use what you learned in this lab to answer the following questions.

1. Bromthymol blue, BTB, is an acid which has a hydrogen ion, H^+, and for the purposes of this question, you will write it HBTB. HBTB ionizes in water to produce hydrogen ion, H^+, and bromthymol blue ion, BTB^-.

$$HBTB \rightleftharpoons H^+ + BTB^-$$

   yellow   blue

   a. What color appeared when you added HCl to BTB? What color is HBTB? Explain the shift in equilibrium in terms of Le Châtelier's principle.

   _____

   _____

   b. What color appeared when you added NaOH to the mixture? What color is BTB^-? Explain the shift in equilibrium in terms of Le Châtelier's principle.

   _____

   _____

   _____

2. Ammonia reacts with water to produce hydroxide ion. Ammonia is neutralized by hydrogen ion:

$$NH_3 + HOH \rightleftharpoons NH_4^+ + OH^-$$

$$NH_3 + H^+ \rightleftharpoons NH_4^+$$

   a. What color did BTB change in the presence of ammonia, NH_3? Explain the color change in terms of Le Châtelier's principle. Include an equation in your explanation.

   _____

   _____

   _____

   b. What happened when HCl was added? Explain in terms of Le Châtelier's principle.

   _____

   _____

3. Copper ions react differently in the presence of varying amounts of ammonia, NH_3. The hydroxide produced from a small amount of ammonia produces a precipitate. Excess ammonia produces a highly colored solution:

$$Cu^{2+} + 2OH^- \rightleftharpoons Cu(OH)_2(s) \text{ (precipitation equilibrium)}$$

$$Cu^{2+} + 4NH_3 \rightleftharpoons Cu(NH_3)_4^{2+} \text{ (complex ion in solution)}$$

a. What color is the *precipitate* when only a little ammonia is added? What color is the *solution* in the presence of excess ammonia?

_____

b. Explain in terms of Le Châtelier's principle the disappearance of the precipitate when excess ammonia is added.

_____

_____

_____

c. What is the effect of the HCl? Explain in terms of Le Châtelier's principle.

_____

_____

_____

_____

_____

4. Lead(II) ion reacts with iodide ion to produce a bright yellow precipitate, and with hydroxide ion to form a milky white precipitate.

$$Pb^{2+} + 2I^- \rightleftharpoons PbI_2(s) \qquad \text{bright yellow}$$

$$Pb^{2+} + 2OH^- \rightleftharpoons Pb(OH)_2(s) \qquad \text{milky white}$$

a. Why does the yellow precipitate disappear when sodium hydroxide is added? Explain in terms of Le Châtelier's principle.

_____

_____

_____

b. Why does the yellow precipitate reappear when nitric acid is added?

_____

_____

_____

5. Lead(II) ion reacts with varying amounts of hydroxide ions in different ways. A small amount of hydroxide produces a precipitate, and excess hydroxide produces a complex ion:

$$Pb^{2+} + 2OH^- \rightleftharpoons Pb(OH)_2(s)$$

$$Pb^{2+} + 3OH^- \rightleftharpoons Pb(OH)_3^- \text{ (complex ion in solution)}$$

a. Why does the precipitate disappear when excess NaOH is added? Explain in terms of Le Châtelier's principle.

_____

_____

_____

b. Why does the precipitate reappear when a little nitric acid is added?

_____

_____

_____

c. Why does the precipitate disappear when excess nitric acid is added?

_____

_____

6. Explain the observations in Step 6 by writing net ionic equations to describe each reaction of silver ion, Ag⁺, you observed.

_____

_____

_____

_____

_____

_____

_____

7. Explain why BTB is green in neutral water solution. In terms of Le Châtelier's principle, why does it turn yellow when acid is added, and blue when base is added?

_____

_____

_____

_____

Name _____ Class _____ Date _____

NOW IT'S YOUR TURN!

1. Repeat Step 1 with other indicators like phenolphthalein, HPhen; bromphenyl blue, HBPB; methyl red, HMR; alizarine yellow R, HAYR; and thymol blue, HTB. Explain in terms of Le Châletier's principle what happens with each when HCl and NaOH are added. Write net ionic equations to describe their reactions in water.

_____

_____

_____

_____

_____

_____

_____

2. Repeat the precipitation reaction of lead nitrate with potassium iodide, as in Step 4. Can you alternately add NaOH and HNO_3 to change the precipitates?

_____

_____

3. Repeat the precipitation reaction of lead nitrate with sodium hydroxide, as in Step 5. Name two ways you can make the precipitate disappear. Prove your answer by carrying out the experiments. Explain.

_____

4. Perform the following experiment and explain your results in terms of Le Châtelier's principle.

$$Fe^{3+} + SCN^- \rightleftharpoons FeSCN^{2+}$$
yellow   blood red
1 drop $FeCl_3$ 1 drop KSCN

1 drop NaOH   1 drop $AgNO_3$
$Fe^{3+} + OH^- \rightleftharpoons Fe(OH)_3(s)$ $Ag^+ + 2SCN^- \rightleftharpoons Ag(SCN)_2^-$

a. Mix 1 drop $FeCl_3$ with 1 drop KSCN. What happened? Write an equation to explain.

_____

b. Add 10 drops water, separate into 4 parts with a soda straw, and add the indicated solutions. Tell what happens in each case. Explain in terms of the respective equilibria.

c. _____

_____

d. _____

_____

e. _____

_____

f. _____

_____

26 A SMALL-SCALE COLORIMETRIC PH METER

Small-Scale Experiment for text section 20.2

OBJECTIVES

- **Construct** and **calibrate** a colorimetric pH meter.
- **Measure** and **record** the pH of various household solutions using the colorimetric pH meter.
- **Calculate** pOH from pH and [H$^+$] and [OH$^-$] from pH and pOH.

INTRODUCTION

pH is a way of expressing how acidic or how basic a solution is. The more acidic a solution is, the lower its pH. The less acidic a solution is, the higher its pH. A pH of 7 represents a neutral solution. A pH lower than 7 is acidic and a pH higher than 7 is basic.

pH is used to express the molar concentration of the acid content of a solution. The relationship between pH and the molar concentration of H$^+$ or [H$^+$] is shown below.

pH	[H+]	Solution Acidity/Basicity
14*	10^{-14}	very basic
13	10^{-13}	
12	10^{-12}	
11	10^{-11}	basic
10	10^{-10}	
9	10^{-9}	
8	10^{-8}	slightly basic
7	10^{-7}	neutral
6	10^{-6}	slightly acidic
5	10^{-5}	
4	10^{-4}	
3	10^{-3}	acidic
2	10^{-2}	
1	10^{-1}	
0*	$10^{-0} = 1$	very acidic

*At these pH's, solutions are not ideal and pH $\neq -\log$[H+].

In summary: If pH > 7, the solution is basic.

If pH = 7, the solution is neutral.

If pH < 7, the solution is acidic.

A pH meter is an instrument used to measure the pH of a solution rapidly and accurately. Most pH meters consist of a pair of electrodes connected to an electronic metering device. A reference electrode has a constant voltage, while a glass electrode changes voltage depending on the pH of the solution being measured. The pH meter compares the difference in voltage between the two electrodes, and this difference is calibrated to read out as a pH. Because pH meters consist of fragile glass electrodes and sensitive electronic parts, they are usually very expensive and often temperamental.

PURPOSE

In this lab you will make a very reliable *calorimetric pH meter*. The colorimetric pH meter uses a *universal indicator*, one that changes color with pH. You will mix the universal indicator with a series of 12 standard pH solutions called *buffers*. Each buffer solution has an integer pH between 1 and 12. In the presence of 12 different buffers, the universal indicator will change to 12 distinctly different colors. You can use these colors as standards by comparing other solutions to them. To measure the pH of an unknown solution, for example, you can add the universal indicator to the solution and match the resulting color with the color of one of the buffers. The pH of the matching buffer is the pH of the unknown solution.

SAFETY ⬤

- Wear your safety glasses.
- Use full small-scale pipets only for the carefully controlled delivery of liquids.

MATERIALS

Small-scale pipets of the following solutions:
universal indicator (UI)
buffer solutions (pH 1–12)
Household products: baking soda, vinegar, window cleaner, baking powder, lemon juice, tea, a cola soft drink, laundry detergent, milk, orange juice, etc.

EQUIPMENT

small-scale reaction surface
empty pipet for stirring

EXPERIMENTAL PAGE

Part A. Constructing a pH Meter

1. Add 1 drop of UI to each space.

2. Add 5 drops of the buffer corresponding to each pH. Stir. Each integer pH should now have a unique and distinguishing color. If not, add more buffer.

pH 1	pH 2	pH 3	pH 4
pH 8	pH 7	pH 6	pH 5
pH 9	pH 10	pH 11	pH 12

Part B. Measuring pH

3. Measure the pHs of various household solutions by placing 5 drops of each liquid to be tested in 1 drop of UI. Stir, and match the color to one of the pHs above.

4. Measure the pHs of various household solids by adding 5 drops of water and 1 drop of UI to a few grains of each solid. Stir, and match the color to one of the pHs above.

Place this side of the Experimental Page facedown. Use the other side under your small-scale reaction surface.

EXPERIMENTAL DATA

Record your results in Tables 26.1 and 26.2 or tables like them in your notebook.

Table 26.1   Colorimetric pH Meter

pH 1	pH 2	pH 3	pH 4
pH 8	pH 7	pH 6	pH 5
pH 9	pH 10	pH 11	pH 12

Table 26.2   pHs of Household Products

Household Product	pH	pH + pOH = 14 pOH	$[H^+] = 10^{-pH}$ $[H^+]$	$[OH^-] = 10^{-pOH}$ $[OH^-]$
vinegar				
window cleaner				
cola				
baking soda				
washing soda				

Calculate the pOH, $[H^+]$, and $[OH^-]$ of each household product you tested, and record your results in Table 26.2.

CLEANING UP

Avoid contamination by cleaning up in a way that protects you and your environment. Carefully clean the small-scale reaction surface by absorbing the contents onto a paper towel. Rinse the reaction surface with a damp paper towel and dry it. Dispose of the paper towels in the waste bin. Wash your hands thoroughly with soap and water.

QUESTIONS FOR ANALYSIS

Use what you learned in this lab to answer the following questions.

1. The relationship between pH and pOH is: pH + pOH = 14. List the pOHs of all the household products you tested.

   _____

   _____

2. The relationship between pH and $[H^+]$ is: $[H^+] = 10^{-pH}$. List the $[H^+]$ of each product you tested.

   _____

   _____

3. The relationship between pOH and $[OH^-]$ is: $[OH^-] = 10^{-pOH}$. List the $[OH^-]$ of each product you tested.

   _____

   _____

4. What limitations does your pH meter have?

   _____

   _____

NOW IT'S YOUR TURN!

1. Search for any other naturally colored substances that can serve as universal indicators. Try flower petals, grape and berry juices, etc.

2. Design an experiment to determine colors of common indicator solutions at various pHs.

   _____

LEWIS ACIDS: ELECTRON PAIR ACCEPTORS

Small-Scale Experiment for text section 20.3

OBJECTIVES

- **Identify** aqueous solutions of metal ions that act as Lewis acids.
- **Determine** which metal ion solutions are the strongest Lewis acids by measuring their pH values.

INTRODUCTION

According to Arrhenius's theory, acids are compounds that ionize in aqueous solution to produce hydrogen ions, while bases ionize to yield hydroxide ions in aqueous solution (Section 20.3). The Brønsted–Lowry theory (Section 20.3) defines an acid as a hydrogen–ion donor and a base as a hydrogen–ion acceptor. Both of these theories require that acids contain hydrogen ions, but there are many examples of acidic compounds that do not contain hydrogen ions.

The Lewis definition of acids includes compounds that do not contain hydrogen ions. A Lewis acid is a substance that accepts a pair of electrons; a Lewis base donates a pair of electrons. Metal ions in aqueous solution often act as Lewis acids. They accept unshared pairs of electrons from water molecules that act as Lewis bases. A Lewis acid may or may not contain hydrogen ions.

PURPOSE

In this lab you will explore the acidic nature of solutions of metal cations to determine which solutions act as Lewis acids. First you will test solutions of metal ions with bromthymol blue and universal indicator to see what colors they produce. Then you will look for evidence of acidic character by mixing these acids with sodium hydrogen carbonate and looking for bubbles. Finally, you will learn to describe the acidic behavior of aqueous metal ions in terms of chemical equations.

SAFETY

- Wear your safety glasses.
- Use full small-scale pipets only for the carefully controlled delivery of liquids.

MATERIALS

Small-scale pipets of the following solutions:

bromthymol blue (BTB)	universal indicator (UI)
sodium hydrogen carbonate ($NaHCO_3$)	sodium chloride (NaCl)
tin(IV) chloride ($SnCl_4$)	calcium chloride ($CaCl_2$)
iron(III) chloride ($FeCl_3$)	potassium chloride (KCl)
zinc chloride ($ZnCl_2$)	aluminum chloride ($AlCl_3$)

silver nitrate ($AgNO_3$)
copper(II) sulfate ($CuSO_4$)
lead(II) nitrate ($Pb(NO_3)_2$)

EQUIPMENT

small-scale reaction surface
empty pipet for stirring

EXPERIMENTAL PAGE

Put 1 drop of each indicated solution in the spaces provided. Observe the color changes in the two indicator solutions, BTB and UI. Watch each $NaHCO_3$ reaction carefully for signs of bubbles. Record your results in Table 27.1.

	BTB	UI	$NaHCO_3$
a. $AlCl_3$ (Al^{3+})			X
b. $CuSO_4$ (Cu^{2+})			X
c. $CaCl_2$ (Ca^{2+})			X
d. $ZnCl_2$ (Zn^{2+})			X
e. $Pb(NO_3)_2$ (Pb^{2+})			X
f. KCl (K^+)			X
g. $FeCl_3$ (Fe^{3+})			X
h. $AgNO_3$ (Ag^+)			X
i. $NaCl$ (Na^+)			X
j. $SnCl_4$ (Sn^{4+})			X

Place this side of the Experimental Page facedown. Use the other side under your small-scale reaction surface.

EXPERIMENTAL DATA

Record your results in Table 27.1 or a table like it in your notebook.

Table 27.1   Lewis Acids

	BTB	UI	NaHCO$_3$
a. AlCl$_3$ (Al^{3+})			
b. CuSO$_4$ (Cu^{2+})			
c. CaCl$_2$ (Ca^{2+})			
d. ZnCl$_2$ (Zn^{2+})			
e. Pb(NO$_3$)$_2$ (Pb^{2+})			
f. KCl (K$^+$)			
g. FeCl$_3$ (Fe^{3+})			
h. AgNO$_3$ (Ag$^+$)			
i. NaCl (Na$^+$)			
j. SnCl$_4$ (Sn^{4+})			

CLEANING UP

Avoid contamination by cleaning up in a way that protects you and your environment. Carefully clean the reaction surface by absorbing the contents onto a paper towel. Rinse it with a damp paper towel and dry it. Dispose of the paper towels in the waste bin. Wash your hands thoroughly with soap and water.

QUESTIONS FOR ANALYSIS

Use what you learned in this lab to answer the following questions.

1. Which aqueous solutions are acids? How do you know?

_____

2. Do any of the acids you listed in Question 1 have a hydrogen ion to donate? How then can any of these compounds be acids?

_____

3. Lewis acids are electron pair acceptors. Metal cations can attract a lone pair of electrons of a water molecule and form a coordinate covalent bond (Section 16.1). These metal cations are electron pair acceptors. For example, Al^{3+} forms a coordinate covalent bond with water:

$$Al^{3+} + H_2O \rightarrow Al(H_2O)^{3+}$$

The resulting ion can now donate a hydrogen ion which can undergo all the usual reactions of acids:

$$Al(H_2O)^{3+} \rightarrow Al(OH)^{2+} + H^+$$

Write equations like the one above for all the metal cations Lewis acid you observed.

_____

_____

_____

_____

_____

4. The best Lewis acids are the metal cations that can most strongly attract electron pairs. In general, should highly positive cations make stronger acids than cations with lower positive charges? Explain.

_____

_____

5. Which cations formed bubbles with $NaHCO_3$? Write a net ionic equation to describe each reaction.

_____

NOW IT'S YOUR TURN!

1. Set up your colorimetric pH meter from Small-Scale Experiment 26, and determine the pH of each acidic solution to the nearest pH unit. Compare the pH values of these metal cation Lewis acids to the pH values of other acids.

_____

2. Which of the cations in the original experiment will most likely form bubbles with $NaHCO_3$? Try some experiments to test your answers! Write a net ionic equation to describe these reactions.

_____

28 STRONG AND WEAK ACIDS AND BASES

Small-Scale Experiment for text section 20.4

OBJECTIVES

- **Identify** and **distinguish between** strong and weak acids and strong and weak bases.
- **Identify** acids and bases as hydrogen–ion acceptors and hydrogen-ion donors.
- **Identify** conjugate acid–base pairs in acid–base reactions.
- **Describe** acid–base reactions by using hydrogen–ion transfer equations.
- **Explain** the differences between strong and weak acids and bases by using equilibrium principles.

INTRODUCTION

You have seen that acids are substances that react with water to produce H_3O^+ ions in solutions. Similarly, bases are chemicals that react with water to produce OH^- ions. For example, you have already seen that when an acid like HCl dissolves in water, it reacts by transferring a hydrogen ion to water according to the following equation:

$$HCl + H_2O \rightarrow H_3O^+ + Cl^-$$

To what degree does this reaction proceed? Do all the molecules of HCl react, or do only some of them transfer hydrogen ions while others remain intact?

PURPOSE

In this lab you will take a new look at acids and bases and classify them according to the Brønsted–Lowry theory. You have already acquired working definitions of acids and bases. Acids turn BTB yellow and produce hydrogen ions in solution. Bases turn BTB blue and produce hydroxide ions in solution. You will use BTB (bromthymol blue) and UI (universal indicator) as probes to classify solutions as acids and bases. You will review how to write net ionic equations to show how each substance transfers a hydrogen ion to or from water. You will learn to identify the acid–base conjugate pairs in hydrogen–ion transfer equations. You will then use the hydrogen carbonate ion, HCO_3^-, to investigate acid–base reactions and group acid solutions according to relative strengths. You will use your data to formulate the concept that acids and bases can be classified as both strong and weak, depending on their behavior.

SAFETY

- Wear your safety glasses.
- Use full small-scale pipets only for the carefully controlled delivery of liquids.

MATERIALS

Small-scale pipets of the following solutions:

sodium hydrogen sulfate (NaHSO$_4$)

sodium hydrogen carbonate (NaHCO$_3$)

sodium dihydrogen phosphate (NaH$_2$PO$_4$)

sodium monohydrogen phosphate (Na$_2$HPO$_4$)

sodium ethanoate (CH$_3$COONa)

universal indicator (UI)

calcium hydroxide (Ca(OH)$_2$)

sodium hydrogen sulfite (NaHSO$_3$)

ethanoic acid (CH$_3$COOH)

sodium carbonate (Na$_2$CO$_3$)

sodium phosphate (Na$_3$PO$_4$)

boric acid (H$_3$BO$_3$)

citric acid (C$_6$H$_8$O$_7$)

ammonium chloride (NH$_4$Cl)

ammonia (NH$_3$)

bromthymol blue (BTB)

nitric acid (HNO$_3$)

hydrochloric acid (HCl)

sulfuric acid (H$_2$SO$_4$)

sodium hydroxide (NaOH)

potassium hydroxide (KOH)

EQUIPMENT

small-scale reaction surface

conductivity apparatus

empty pipet for stirring

EXPERIMENTAL PAGE

Part A. Acids and Indicators

1. Mix 1 drop of each indicated solution. Look carefully for similarities and differences to distinguish strong acids from weak acids.

2. Test each acid for conductivity. Be sure to rinse the leads of the conductivity apparatus between tests. Record your results in Table 28.1.

1 drop of each acid

	HCl	HNO$_3$	H$_2$SO$_4$	2 drops HCl + 9 drops H$_2$O	CH$_3$COOH	citric acid C$_6$H$_8$O$_7$	boric acid H$_3$BO$_3$
1 drop each BTB							
UI							
Na$_2$CO$_3$							
Test for conductivity							

Part B. Acids, Bases, and Indicators

3. Mix 1 drop of indicator with 5 drops of each of the indicated solutions. Record your results in Table 28.2.

	1 drop each BTB	1 drop each UI		1 drop each BTB	1 drop each UI		1 drop each BTB	UI
5 drops each NaHSO$_4$ (HSO$_4^-$)			NaHCO$_3$ (HCO$_3^-$)			Ca(OH)$_2$ (OH$^-$)		
NaOH (OH$^-$)			Na$_2$CO$_3$ (CO$_3^{2-}$)			CH$_3$COONa (CH$_3$COO$^-$)		
Na$_2$HPO$_4$ (HPO$_4^{2-}$)			NaH$_2$PO$_4$ (H$_2$PO$_4^-$)			Na$_3$PO$_4$ (PO$_4^{3-}$)		
KOH (OH$^-$)			NaHSO$_3$ (HSO$_3^-$)			NH$_3$		

Name _____ Class _____ Date _____

EXPERIMENTAL DATA

Record your results in Tables 28.1 and 28.2 or tables like them in your notebook.

Table 28.1 Acids and Indicators

	HCl	HNO$_3$	H$_2$SO$_4$	2 drops HCl + 9 drops H$_2$O	CH$_3$COOH	citric acid C$_6$H$_8$O$_7$	boric acid H$_3$BO$_3$
BTB							
UI							
Na$_2$CO$_3$							
Test for conductivity							

Table 28.2 Acids, Bases, and Indicators

1 drop each   1 drop each

1 drop each

	BTB	UI		BTB	UI		BTB	UI
NaHSO$_4$ (HSO$_4^-$)			NaHCO$_3$ (HCO$_3^-$)			Ca(OH)$_2$ (OH$^-$)		
NaOH (OH$^-$)			Na$_2$CO$_3$ (CO$_3^{2-}$)			CH$_3$COONa (CH$_3$COO$^-$)		
Na$_2$HPO$_4$ (HPO$_4^{2-}$)			NaH$_2$PO$_4$ (H$_2$PO$_4^-$)			Na$_3$PO$_4$ (PO$_4^{3-}$)		
KOH (OH$^-$)			NaHSO$_3$ (HSO$_3^-$)			NH$_3$		

Name _____ Class _____ Date _____

CLEANING UP

Avoid contamination by cleaning up in a way that protects you and your environment. Carefully clean the small-scale reaction surface by absorbing the contents onto a paper towel, wipe the reaction surface with a damp paper towel, and dry it. Dispose of the paper towels in the waste bin. Wash your hands thoroughly with soap and water.

QUESTIONS FOR ANALYSIS

Use what you learned in this lab to answer the following questions.

1. What does BTB indicate that all solutions in Part A can be classified as?

_____

2. What is the chemical behavior of all the solutions with Na_2CO_3? Is this typical of acids or bases?

_____

3. Suggest a reason that the acids give different colors with universal indicator.

_____

_____

_____

4. Which HCl reaction does the ethanoic acid reaction more closely resemble? Why does the undiluted HCl seem to be a "stronger" acid than ethanoic acid?

_____

_____

5. To account for the different rates of reaction with Na_2CO_3, predict which acid, HCl or ethanoic, probably has the greater amount of hydrogen ions present in solution. Do both acids transfer hydrogen ions to water to the same degree? Which ionizes to the greater degree?

_____

6. Classify each solution in Part B as an acid or a base. Estimate the pH of each solution and classify each as strong or weak. For all the weak acids and bases, write a net ionic equation to describe the hydrogen–ion transfer reaction of each acid or base with water. (Show each acid as a hydrogen–ion donor and each base as a hydrogen-ion acceptor.)
For example:

An acid is a *hydrogen–ion donor:* $CH_3COOH + HOH \rightleftharpoons H_3O^+ + CH_3COO^-$

A base is a *hydrogen–ion acceptor:* $NH_3 + HOH \rightleftharpoons NH_4^+ + OH^-$

Notice that water acts as a base in the first equation and as an acid in the second. Water is said to be *amphoteric* because it can act as an acid or base, depending on the conditions. As always, when writing net ionic equations, you can ignore Na^+ ions because they are spectator ions.

_____

_____

_____

_____

_____

_____

_____

_____

_____

_____

7. Identify each pair of species in your net ionic equations (both reactants and products) as a conjugate acid–base pair. For example:

$$NH_3 + HOH \rightleftharpoons NH_4^+ + OH^{-1}$$

conjugate acid–base pair

acid   base

base   acid

conjugate acid–base pair

_____

_____

_____

NOW IT'S YOUR TURN!

1. Investigate the common chemical solutions in this lab for use in a colorimetric pH meter in place of pH buffer standards. Set up the pH meter as in Small-Scale Experiment 26, and match the colors various solutions produce with UI.

2. Design an experiment to use hydrogen carbonate ion, HCO_3^-, as a probe for weak acids. For example, you have seen that carbonates react with acids to produce carbon dioxide and water:

$$CO_3^{2-} + 2H^+ \rightleftharpoons CO_2(g) + H_2O$$

Notice that the stoichiometry of the reaction requires 2 moles of hydrogen ions for every 1 mole of carbonate. If the amount of available hydrogen ion were limited, say, by the presence of a weak acid, the reaction might produce hydrogen carbonate ion rather than carbon dioxide:

$$CO_3^{2-} + H^+ \rightleftharpoons HCO_3^-$$

An additional equivalent of hydrogen ion is needed to carry the reaction to completion:

$$HCO_3^- + H^+ \rightleftharpoons CO_2(g) + H_2O$$

29 TITRATION CURVES

Small-Scale Experiment for text section 21.1

OBJECTIVES

- **Observe** and **record** pH changes during various acid–base titrations.
- **Construct** titration curves from experimental data for these titrations.
- **Interpret** titration curves and identify suitable indicators for the titrations.
- **Estimate** the pKs of various weak acids and bases.

INTRODUCTION

You have already learned that acid–base indicators are weak acids or bases that change color near their pKs. Because the accuracy of a titration depends in part on how closely the end point coincides with the equivalence point, the indicator used should change color very near the equivalence point. Phenolphthalein changes form colorless to pink in basic solution at about pII 9, yet we used this indicator to detect the end points of acid–base titrations that have equivalence points at exactly pH 7. How can you tell if phenolphthalein is a suitable indicator for the titrations of strong acids with strong bases? You can answer this question by examining the nature of titration curves.

A *titration curve* is a graph showing how the pH changes as a function of the amount of added titrant in a titration. You obtain data for a titration curve by titrating a solution and measuring the pH after every drop of added titrant. For example, you can construct a titration curve for the titration of hydrochloric acid with sodium hydroxide, NaOH, by measuring the pH after every drop of NaOH. A plot of the pH on the y-axis versus drops of NaOH on the x-axis will tell us how the pH changes as the titration proceeds.

A titration curve gives you a lot of information about a titration. For example, you can use the curve to identify the pH of the *equivalence point* of the titration. The equivalence point is the point on the titration curve where the moles of acid equal the moles of base. The midpoint of the steepest part of the curve (the most abrupt change in pH) is a good approximation of the equivalence point.

You can use knowledge of the equivalence point to choose a suitable indicator for a given titration. The indicator must change color at a pH that corresponds to the equivalence point. Because all titrations of weak acids and bases are different, it is important to construct titration curves and choose suitable indicators before you try to determine the concentrations of weak acids and bases.

Finally, you can use your titration curves to approximate the pKs of various weak acids and bases. Ethanoic acid, for example, ionizes in water to a small extent according to the following equation:

$$CH_3COOH + H_2O \rightleftharpoons CH_3COO^- + H_3O^+$$

The acid ionization constant, K_a, is expressed as:

$$K_a = \frac{[CH_3COO^-][H_3O^+]}{[CH_3COOH]}$$

When the acid is exactly half neutralized (half the number of drops of NaOH to the equivalence point), $[CH_3COOH] = [CH_3COO^-]$. So $K_a = [H_3O^+]$ or $pK_a = pH$. This means that the pH of the solution halfway to the equivalence point represents a good approximation of the pK_a.

PURPOSE

In this lab you will use your colorimetric pH meter from Small-Scale Experiment 26 to generate data to construct the titration curves for various acid–base titrations. You will use the information obtained from the graphs to estimate the pKs of various weak acids and bases and to choose the appropriate indicator for each titration.

SAFETY

- Wear your safety glasses.
- Use full small-scale pipets only for the carefully controlled delivery of liquids.

MATERIALS

Small-scale pipets of the following solutions:
buffer solutions (pH 1–12)   universal indicator (UI)
ethanoic acid (CH$_3$COOH)

hydrochloric acid (HCl)

sodium hydroxide (NaOH)

EQUIPMENT

plastic cups
small-scale reaction surface
empty pipet for stirring

EXPERIMENTAL PAGE

1. Construct a pH meter for use in this experiment: Place 1 drop of UI in each space below, then add 5 drops of each indicated pH solution. Record your data in Table 29.1.

pH 1	pH 2	pH 3	pH 4
pH 8	pH 7	pH 6	pH 5
pH 9	pH 10	pH 11	pH 12

2. Add 1 drop of UI and 4 drops of HCl to each of the following spaces. Then add the indicated number of drops of NaOH while stirring. Record the pH of each mixture in Table 29.2.

1 drop NaOH	2 drops NaOH	3 drops NaOH	4 drops NaOH
8 drops NaOH	7 drops NaOH	6 drops NaOH	5 drops NaOH
9 drops NaOH	10 drops NaOH	11 drops NaOH	12 drops NaOH

3. Repeat Step 2 on a larger scale in a cup. Add 1 drop of UI and 10 drops of HCl to a clean, dry cup. Add NaOH drop by drop, and record the pH after each drop in Table 29.1. Continue for 25 to 30 drops of NaOH.

4. Repeat Step 3, using CH_3COOH. Add 1 drop of UI and 10 drops of CH_3COOH to a clean, dry cup. Add NaOH drop by drop, and record the pH after each drop in Table 29.1. Continue for 25 to 30 drops of NaOH.

Name _____ Class _____ Date _____

EXPERIMENTAL DATA

Record your results in Tables 29.1 and 29.2 or in tables like them in your notebook.

Table 29.1 Colorimetric pH Meter

pH 1	pH 2	pH 3	pH 4
pH 8	pH 7	pH 6	pH 5
pH 9	pH 10	pH 11	pH 12

Table 29.2 Titration

Drops of NaOH and corresponding pHs

HCl/NaOII (reaction surface)	Drops	1	2	3	4	5	6	7	8	9	10	11	12
	pH												

HCl/NaOH (cup)	Drops	1	2	3	4	5	6	7	8	9	10	11	12
	pH												
	Drops	13	14	15	16	17	18	19	20	21	22	23	24
	pH												
	Drops	25	26	27	28	29	30						
	pH												

CH₃COOH/NaOH (cup)	Drops	1	2	3	4	5	6	7	8	9	10	11	12
	pH												
	Drops	13	14	15	16	17	18	19	20	21	22	23	24
	pH												
	Drops	25	26	27	28	29	30						
	pH												

Name _____ Class _____ Date _____

Use graph paper to construct a titration curve for both titrations, HCl and CH_3COOH, by plotting the pH (y-axis) versus the number of drops of NaOH added (x-axis). Connect the points with a smooth "S" curve.

CLEANING UP

Avoid contamination by cleaning up in a way that protects you and your environment. Carefully clean the reaction surface by absorbing the contents onto a paper towel, wipe it with a damp paper towel, and dry it. Clean the plastic cup by disposing of the liquid contents and rinsing it thoroughly with water. Dry it with a paper towel. Dispose of the paper towels in the waste bin. Wash your hands thoroughly with soap and water.

QUESTIONS FOR ANALYSIS

Use what you learned in this lab to answer the following questions.

1. Write and balance a chemical equation to describe the reaction between HCl and NaOH. What is the mole ratio between HCl and NaOH?

    _____

2. Write and balance a chemical equation to describe the reaction between CH_3COOH and NaOH. What is the mole ratio between CH_3COOH and NaOH?

    _____

3. The equivalence point is the point on the titration curve where the moles of acid equal the moles of base. The pH of the equivalence point of the titration can be approximated by finding the midpoint of the steepest part of the graph (where the pH changes most rapidly). Examine your titration curve for the titration of HCl with NaOH in the cup. What is the pH at the equivalence point for the titration?

    _____

4. Examine your titration curve for the titration of CH_3COOH with NaOH. What is the pH at the equivalence point for the titration?

_____

5. You can use your knowledge of the equivalence point to choose a suitable indicator for any acid–base titration. The indicator must change color at a pH that is at the steepest part of the titration curve. Examine your titration curve of HCl with NaOH, and explain why a large number of indicators would be suitable for this titration.

_____

_____

6. Choose suitable indicators for this titration from your data in Small-Scale Experiment 28.

_____

7. Choose a suitable indicator for the titration of CH_3COOH with NaOH from your data in Small-Scale Experiment 28.

_____

8. Compare the general shape of the curve for the weak acid (CH_3COOH) with the one for the strong acid (HCl).

a. Which curve has a higher initial pH?

_____

b. Which curve rises faster near the equivalence point?

_____

c. Is the pH at the equivalence point the same for both?

_____

d. Will the same group of indicators detect both equivalence points?

_____

9. You can use your titration curve to approximate the pK_a of ethanoic acid (CH_3COOH). Ethanoic acid ionizes in water to a small extent, according to the following equation:

$$CH_3COOH + H_2O \rightleftharpoons CH_3COO^- + H_3O^+$$

The acid ionization constant, K_a, is expressed as:

$$K_a = \frac{[CH_3COO^-][H_3O^+]}{[CH_3COOH]}$$

When the acid is exactly half-neutralized (half the number of drops of NaOH to the equivalence point), then half of the ethnaoic acid has been converted to acetate ion. This means that the amount of ethanoic acid left equals the amount of acetate ion produced, or $[CH_3COOH] = [CH_3COO^-]$. These values cancel in the above expression, resulting in $K_a = [H_3O^+]$ or $pK_a = pH$. This means that the pH of the solution halfway to the equivalence point represents a good approximation of the pK_a. At the equivalence point, how many drops of NaOH are required?

_____

10. What is the pH of the solution when half that many drops have been added? Estimate the pK_a of ethanoic acid.

_____

11. If NaOH is 0.5M, use your titration data to calculate the approximate molar concentration of HCl and CH_3COOH. Assume that the drop sizes are the same and that they are proportional to liters.

NOW IT'S YOUR TURN!

1. Repeat Step 3 on the Experimental Page, using HNO_3 instead of HCl. Add 1 drop of UI and 10 drops of HNO_3 to a clean, dry cup. Add NaOH drop by drop, and record the pH after each drop. Continue for 25 to 30 drops of NaOH. Record your observations. Construct a titration curve.

2. Design experiments to construct titration curves for the titrations of the following: H_2SO_4 with NaOH, H_3PO_4 with NaOH, Na_2CO_3 with HCl, and NH_3 with HCl.

3. Repeat all four titrations, but this time do them "backwards." For HCl, HNO_3, and CH_3COOH, add 20 drops of NaOH first and then titrate with the acid. Record the pH after each drop, and construct titration curves. For NH_3, add 10 drops of HCl and titrate with NH_3.

BUFFERS

Small-Scale Experiment for text section 21.2

OBJECTIVES

- **Measure** and **record** the pHs of various buffer solutions.
- **Determine** the resistance of various buffers to changes in pH.

INTRODUCTION

A *buffer solution* is a solution that resists a change in pH when small amounts of acid or base are added to it. Buffer solutions are usually composed of a conjugate acid–base pair—either a weak acid and the salt of its conjugate base or a weak base and the salt of its conjugate acid. For example, a buffer that maintains a pH of about 4.5 can be prepared by making a solution of ethanoic acid and sodium acetate.

$$CH_3COOH + H_2O \rightleftharpoons H_3O^+ + CH_3COO^-$$
acid   base
                               (from sodium acetate)

$$CH_3COO^- + H_2O \rightleftharpoons CH_3COOH + OH^-$$
base   acid
(from sodium acetate)

Such a mixture resists a change in pH because the weak acid, CH_3COOH, will react with any added base. Similarly, the base, CH_3COO^-, will react with added acid.

A buffer can also be made of a weak base and the salt of its conjugate acid. Ammonia and ammonium chloride, for example, make up a buffer that maintains a pH of about 10.

$$NH_3 + H_2O \rightleftharpoons NH_4^+ + OH^-$$
base   acid

This buffer also has an acid and a base that are capable of reacting with added hydronium or hydroxide ions to maintain the pH at a nearly constant value.

PURPOSE

In this lab you will prepare several buffer solutions. You will add small amounts of both acid and base to each buffer to test their resistance to change in pH. You will then design other buffer solutions from weak acids and weak bases and test their behavior toward added acid and base.

SAFETY

- Wear your safety glasses.
- Use full small-scale pipets only for the carefully controlled delivery of liquids.

MATERIALS

Small-scale pipets of the following solutions:

ethanoic acid (CH$_3$COOH)

ammonia (NH$_3$)

sodium carbonate (Na$_2$CO$_3$)

sodium chloride (NaCl)

sodium nitrate (NaNO$_3$)

sodium sulfate (Na$_2$SO$_4$)

universal indicator (UI)

sodium ethaoate (CH$_3$COONa)

ammonium chloride (NH$_4$Cl)

sodium hydrogen carbonate (NaHCO$_3$)

sodium dihydrogen phosphate (NaH$_2$PO$_4$)

potassium iodide (KI)

water (H$_2$O)

buffer solution (pH 1–12)

sodium hydroxide (NaOH)

hydrochloric acid (HCl)

phosphoric acid (H$_3$PO$_4$)

EQUIPMENT

3 plastic cups

small-scale reaction surface

EXPERIMENTAL PAGE

1. Construct a pH meter for use in this experiment: Place 1 drop of UI in each space below, then 5 drops of each indicated pH solution.

pH 1	pH 2	pH 3	pH 4
pH 8	pH 7	pH 6	pH 5
pH 9	pH 10	pH 11	pH 12

2. Place 3 cups in the designated places, and add 1 drop of UI and 10 drops of distilled H_2O to each.

1 drop UI

1 drop UI

1 drop UI

Count the number of drops of NaOH to a distinct color change.

Count the number of drops of HCl to a distinct color change.

Use a control to compare colors.

3. Place 3 cups in the designated places and add 1 drop of UI, 10 drops of CH_3COOH, and 10 drops of CH_3COONa to each.

1 drop UI

1 drop UI

1 drop UI

Count the number of drops of NaOH to a distinct color change.

Count the number of drops of HCl to a distinct color change.

Use a control to compare colors.

4. Repeat Step 3, replacing the CH_3COOH and CH_3COONa, in turn, with the following combinations.

a. $H_3PO_4 + NaH_2PO_4$ b. $NaHCO_3 + Na_2CO_3$ c. $NH_4Cl + NH_3$

d. $NaCl + NaNO_3$ e. $Na_2SO_4 + KI$ f. $H_3PO_4 + NaOH$

g. Try mixing various combinations and test their buffer capacities.

Place this side of the Experimental Page facedown. Use the other side under your small-scale reaction surface.

Name _____ Class _____ Date _____

EXPERIMENTAL DATA

Record your results in Tables 30.1 and 30.2 or tables like them in your notebook.

Table 30.1   Colorimetric pH Meter

pH 1	pH2	pH 3	pH 4
pH 8	pH 7	pH 6	pH 5
pH 9	pH 10	pH 11	pH 12

Table 30.2   Buffers

Mixture	Initial pH	Drops NaOH to change	Drops HCl to change
H_2O			
$CH_3COOH + CH_3COONa$			
$H_3PO_4 + NaH_2PO_4$			
$NaHCO_3 + Na_2CO_3$			
$NH_4Cl + NH_3$			
$NaCl + NaNO_3$			
$Na_2SO_4 + KI$			
$H_3PO_4 + NaOH$			

CLEANING UP

Avoid contamination by cleaning up in a way that protects you and your environment. Carefully clean the reaction surface by absorbing the contents onto a paper towel, wipe it with a damp paper towel, and dry it. Clean the plastic cups by disposing of the liquid contents and rinsing them thoroughly with water. Dry them with a paper towel. Dispose of the paper towels in the waste bin. Wash your hands thoroughly with soap and water.

Name _____ Class _____ Date _____

QUESTIONS FOR ANALYSIS

Use what you learned in this lab to answer the following questions.

1. What is a buffer?

   _____

2. How do you know which mixtures are buffers?

   _____

3. How do you know which mixtures are not buffers?

   _____

4. Buffer capacity is a measure of the amount of acid or base a buffer will absorb before it changes pH significantly. A crude measure of buffer capacity is the number of drops of acid or base that is added before a pH change is shown by an indicator color change. What is the buffer capacity of each solution you measured in this experiment?

   _____

   _____

NOW IT'S YOUR TURN!

1. Use the chemicals in this lab to explore other possible buffer combinations. Mix 10 drops each of various solutions, two at a time, and test the buffer capacity of each resulting solution. Tell what you mix and what happens in each case.

   _____

   _____

2. Buffers are mixtures of weak acids and bases. Because of their formulations, some common household products are potential buffers. Design and carry out experiments to test household products for buffer capacity. Tell what you do and what the results are. Whenever possible, read the label of each product to try to determine the chemicals that give the substance its buffer capacity.

   _____

   _____

   _____

   _____

   _____

   _____

31 DETERMINATION OF AN ACTIVITY SERIES

Small-Scale Experiment for text section 22.1

OBJECTIVES

- **Derive** an activity series from experimental data.
- **Describe** oxidation–reduction reactions by writing net ionic equations and half-reactions.
- **Formulate** a functional definition for "oxidation" and "reduction."

INTRODUCTION

You have seen that magnesium reacts with HCl much more readily than does zinc. Copper appears not to react at all with hydrochloric acid. The half-reactions that describe these processes reveal that electrons are lost by the metals and gained by the hydrogen ions. For example, the half-reactions for the reaction of magnesium with hydrochloric acid are

$$2H^+ + 2e^- \rightarrow H_2(g) \qquad \text{reduction}$$

$$Mg(s) \rightarrow Mg^{2+} + 2e^- \qquad \text{oxidation}$$

The relative ease with which a metal loses electrons is called its *oxidation potential*. You have seen, for example, that magnesium is more reactive toward acids than is zinc. This means that magnesium loses electrons more readily than zinc does. In other words, magnesium has a higher oxidation potential.

Conversely, the relative ease with which a metal cation gains electrons is called its *reduction potential*. For example, we have seen that copper ions react with zinc metal according to the following half-reactions and net ionic equation:

Reduction	$Cu^{2+} + 2e^- \rightarrow Cu(s)$
Oxidation	$Zn(s) \rightarrow Zn^{2+} + 2e^-$
Net ionic	$Cu^{2+} + Zn(s) \rightarrow Cu(s) + Zn^{2+}$

Because copper ions react with zinc metal by taking away its electrons, we can say that copper has the greater reduction potential and zinc has the greater oxidation potential.

PURPOSE

In this lab you will carry out a series of reactions in which electrons are gained and lost between metals and metal ions. You will organize the experiments so that metals actually compete for each other's electrons. You will observe which metals lose electrons more readily and which metal ions gain electrons more readily. You can compare the relative tendencies of metals to gain and lose electrons by counting the number of reactions each metal and each metal ion undergoes. The metal involved in the most reactions is the one that loses electrons (is oxidized) the most readily. It has the highest oxidation potential. The metal involved in the least number of reactions loses electrons the least readily. It has the lowest oxidation potential. A list of metals ranging from those most easily oxidized to those least easily oxidized is called an activity series. From this data you will derive an activity series for common metals.

SAFETY

- Wear your safety glasses.
- Use full small-scale pipets only for the carefully controlled delivery of liquids.

MATERIALS

Small-scale pipets of the following solutions:
iron(II) sulfate (FeSO$_4$)   magnesium sulfate (MgSO$_4$)
zinc chloride (ZnCl$_2$)

silver nitrate (AgNO$_3$)
copper(II) sulfate (CuSO$_4$)

Four pieces each of the following solid metals:
zinc (Zn)   iron (Fe)
magnesium (Mg)   silver (Ag)
copper (Cu)

EQUIPMENT

small-scale reaction surface

EXPERIMENTAL PAGE

Add 2 drops of each salt solution to one piece of each of the indicated metals.

	$CuSO_4$ (Cu^{2+})	$FeSO_4$ (Fe^{2+})	$MgSO_4$ (Mg^{2+})	$AgNO_3$ (Ag^+)	$ZnCl_2$ (Zn^{2+})
1 piece each Zn(s)					■
Ag(s)				■	
Mg(s)			■		
Fe(s)		■			
Cu(s)	■				

Place this side of the Experimental Page facedown. Use the other side under your small-scale reaction surface.

EXPERIMENTAL DATA

Record your results in Table 31.1 or a table like it in your notebook.

Table 31.1   Metal Activity

	$CuSO_4$ (Cu^{2+})	$FeSO_4$ (Fe^{2+})	$MgSO_4$ (Mg^{2+})	$AgNO_3$ (Ag^+)	$ZnCl_2$ (Zn^{2+})	
Zn(s)					■	_____ _____
Ag(s)				■		_____ _____
Mg(s)			■			_____ _____
Fe(s)		■				_____ _____
Cu(s)	■					_____ _____

Write oxidation and reduction half-reactions for each metal in the spaces provided next to the table.

CLEANING UP

Avoid contamination by cleaning up in a way that protects you and your environment. Carefully clean and dry each piece of leftover metal and place it in the appropriate recycling container. Clean the reaction surface by absorbing the contents onto a paper towel, rinse it with a damp paper towel, and dry it. Dispose of the paper towels in the waste bin. Wash your hands thoroughly with soap and water.

Name _____ Class _____ Date _____

QUESTIONS FOR ANALYSIS

Use what you learned in this lab to answer the following questions.

1. Read across each row of Table 31.1. Count the number of reactions that each metal undergoes with the metal salts. Order them according to reactivity. This order is called an activity series.

_____

2. Reading down the rows of Table 31.1, count the number of reactions that each metal ion undergoes. Order them according to reactivity.

_____

3. Compare the reactivity of the metal ions to that of the metals. What are the similarities and differences?

_____

_____

4. For each reaction you observe, a metal is oxidized; that is, it gives away its electrons. In doing so, the metal becomes a metal ion. Write an oxidation half-reaction for each reaction you observed. Write them in order of reactivity, with the most reactive first.

_____

_____

_____

_____

_____

5. For each reaction you observe, a metal ion is reduced; that is, the metal ion gains electrons. In doing so, the metal ion becomes a metal atom. Write a reduction half-reaction for each reaction you observed. Write them in order of reactivity, with the most reactive first.

_____

_____

_____

_____

_____

6. Examine your two lists of half-reactions and describe how each list can be used to predict whether a reaction will occur between a metal and a metal ion.

_____

_____

_____

Name _____ Class _____ Date _____

7. Add the half-reactions to obtain the net ionic equations for each of the reactions you observed. Use either list and choose two half-reactions. Reverse the one lower on the list and add them together. Make sure the number of electrons gained equals the number of electrons lost. For example,

Oxidation $Mg^0(s) \rightarrow Mg^{2+} + 2e^-$
Reduction $2\,[Ag^+ + e^- \rightarrow Ag^0(s)]$
_____
Net Ionic Equation $Mg^0(s) + 2Ag^+ \rightarrow Mg^{2+} + 2Ag^0(s)$

Notice that silver metal does not give its electrons to a zinc ion:

$Ag^0(s) + Zn^{2+} \rightarrow$ No Visible Reaction

_____

_____

_____

_____

_____

_____

_____

_____

_____

NOW IT'S YOUR TURN!

1. Repeat the experiment, using common household objects in place of the metals. For example, use galvanized nails or zinc-plated washers for zinc, silverware for silver, staples for iron, and pennies for copper. How do your results compare with the original experiment?

_____

32 OXIDATION–REDUCTION REACTIONS

Small-Scale Experiment for text section 22.3

OBJECTIVES

- **Observe** and **record** oxidation–reduction reactions between aqueous ions.
- **Describe** oxidation and reduction processes by writing half-reactions.
- **Write** and balance redox equations by balancing half-reactions.
- **Identify** reactants as oxidizing agents and reducing agents.

INTRODUCTION

You saw in the last two labs that oxidation–reduction reactions commonly occur when metals react with either acids or metal ions. Redox reactions also occur between ions, one ion being oxidized and the other being reduced. For example, permanganate ions, MnO_4^-, undergo a redox reaction with iodide ions, I^-, in the presence of acid:

$$16H^+ + 2MnO_4^- + 10I^- \rightarrow 2Mn^{2+} + 5I_2 + 8H_2O$$

This reaction is easily seen in the laboratory because permanganate has a distinctive purple color that disappears upon formation of the nearly colorless Mn^{2+} ion. Similarly, the colorless iodide ion reacts to form the iodine molecule, which appears yellow in aqueous solution. The reaction mixture turns from purple to yellow as the reaction proceeds.

In this reaction, permanganate is reduced and iodide is oxidized. In other words, manganese gains electrons and iodine loses electrons. Because permanganate accepts electrons from iodide and causes iodide to be oxidized, permanganate, the reduced reactant, is also called the oxidizing agent. Similarly, because iodide donates electrons to permanganate and causes permanganate to be reduced, iodide, the oxidized reactant, is also called a reducing agent.

PURPOSE

In this lab you will carry out a number of redox reactions involving ions in aqueous solution and write balanced equations to describe the reactions. You will also identify the oxidizing and reducing agents in each case and become familiar with which substances usually act as oxidizing agents and which are most often reducing agents.

SAFETY 🥽

- Wear your safety glasses.
- Use full small-scale pipets only for the carefully controlled delivery of liquids.

MATERIALS

Small-scale pipets of the following solutions:

potassium iodide (KI)

sodium hydrogen sulfite ($NaHSO_3$)

iron(III) chloride ($FeCl_3$)

sodium hydrogen sulfate ($NaHSO_4$)

hydrogen peroxide (H_2O_2)

sodium nitrite ($NaNO_2$)

starch solution

sodium thiosulfate ($Na_2S_2O_3$)

sodium hypochlorite (NaOCl)

potassium permanganate ($KMnO_4$)

potassium iodate (KIO_3)

potassium dichromate ($K_2Cr_2O_7$)

copper(II) sulfate ($CuSO_4$)

hydrochloric acid (HCl)

EQUIPMENT

small-scale reaction surface

EXPERIMENTAL PAGE

1. Mix 1 drop each of the indicated solutions in the spaces below. If no reaction is visible, add starch, an indicator for I_2. If no reaction occurs still, add HCl. Record your results in Table 32.1.

KI
(I^-)

a. NaOCl (OCl^-)
$$OCl^- + I^- \rightarrow Cl^- + I_2$$

b. $KMnO_4$ (MnO_4^-)
$$MnO_4^- + I^- \rightarrow Mn^{2+} + I_2$$

c. H_2O_2
$$H_2O_2 + I^- \rightarrow H_2O + I_2$$

d. KIO_3 (IO_3^-)
$$IO_3^- + I^- \rightarrow I^- + I_2$$

e. $K_2Cr_2O_7$ ($Cr_2O_7^{2-}$)
$$Cr_2O_7^{2-} + I^- \rightarrow Cr^{3+} + I_2$$

f. $NaNO_2$ (NO_2^-)
$$NO_2 + I^- \rightarrow NO(g) + I_2$$

g. $CuSO_4$ (Cu^{2+})
$$Cu^{2+} + I^- \rightarrow CuI(s) + I_2$$

h. $FeCl_3$ (Fe^{3+})
$$Fe^{3+} + I^- \rightarrow Fe^{2+} I_2$$

2. Add a few drops of $NaHSO_3$ to each of the mixtures in Step 1, a–d. Record your results in Table 32.1.

$$HSO_3^- + I_2 \rightarrow SO_4^{2-} + I^-$$

3. Add a few drops of $Na_2S_2O_3$ to each of the mixtures in Step 1, e–h. Record your results in Table 32.1.

$$S_2O_3^{2-} + I_2 \rightarrow S_4O_6^{2-} + I^-$$

Place this side of the Experimental Page facedown. Use the other side under your small-scale reaction surface.

Name _____ Class _____ Date _____

EXPERIMENTAL DATA

Record your results in Table 32.1 or a table like it in your notebook.

Table 32.1   Redox Reactions and Indicators

	KI	Starch	HCl	NaHSO$_3$	Na$_2$S$_2$O$_3$
a. NaOCl					
b. KMnO$_4$					
c. H$_2$O$_2$					
d. KIO$_3$					
e. K$_2$Cr$_2$O$_7$					
f. NaNO$_2$					
g. CuSO$_4$					
h. FeCl$_3$					

CLEANING UP

Avoid contamination by cleaning up in a way that protects you and your environment. Carefully clean the reaction surface by absorbing the contents onto a paper towel, wipe it with a damp paper towel, and dry it. Dispose of the paper towels in the waste bin. Wash your hands thoroughly with soap and water.

QUESTIONS FOR ANALYSIS

Use what you learned in this lab to answer the following questions.

1. What color is aqueous I_2? What color is I_2 in the presence of starch?

_____

2. Listed below are the reactants and products for each mixing. Assign oxidation numbers to each chemical species that changes oxidation number and then write half-reactions for each reaction.

a. $OCl^- + I^- \rightarrow Cl^- + I_2$

_____

_____

e. $Cr_2O_7^{2-} + I^- \rightarrow Cr^{3+} + I_2$

_____

_____

b. $MnO_4^- + I^- \rightarrow Mn^{2+} + I_2$

_____

_____

f. $NO_2^- + I^- \rightarrow NO(g) + I_2$

_____

_____

c. $H_2O_2 + I^- \rightarrow H_2O + I_2$

_____

_____

g. $Cu^{2+} + I^- \rightarrow CuI(s) + I_2$

_____

_____

d. $IO_3^- + I^- \rightarrow I^- + I_2$

_____

_____

h. $Fe^{3+} + I^- \rightarrow Fe^{2+} + I_2$

_____

_____

(*Remember:* Half-reactions must be balanced only for the chemical species that gains or loses electrons.)

3. What color did the mixtures turn upon addition of $NaHSO_3$? $Na_2S_2O_3$? What does each indicate?

_____

_____

4. Given the reactants and products for Steps 2 and 3, write half-reactions for each:

$HSO_3^- + I_2 \rightarrow SO_4^{2-} + I^-$

_____

_____

$S_2O_3^{2-} + I_2 \rightarrow S_4O_6^{2-} + I^-$

_____

_____

5. Fill in the table below with all of the oxidizing agents and reducing agents that you observed in this experiment.

Oxidizing agents	Reducing agents	Oxidizing agents	Reducing agents

6. Complete and balance redox equations for each reaction you observed. Multiply each half-reaction by coefficients that balance the electrons gained and lost, and add the half-reactions. For example,

$$2\,[MnO_4^- + 5e^- \rightarrow Mn^{2+}]$$
$$\underline{5\,[2I^- \rightarrow I_2 + 2e^-]}$$
$$2MnO_4^- + 10I^- \rightarrow 2Mn^{2+} + 5I_2$$

Add water to one side of the equation to balance the oxygens, and add H^+ to the other side to balance the hydrogens:

$$16H^+ + 2MnO_4^- + 10I^- \rightarrow 2Mn^{2+} + 5I_2 + 8H_2O$$

Check to see that all atoms are balanced and that the total charge is balanced.

_____

_____

_____

_____

_____

_____

_____

_____

NOW IT'S YOUR TURN!

1. Recall that an *oxidizing agent* is a chemical that causes another chemical to be oxidized, and in the process the oxidizing agent is reduced (gains electrons). Similarly, a *reducing agent* is a chemical that causes another chemical to be reduced, and in the process the reducing agent is oxidized (loses electrons). For example, in this lab you observed that OCl^- is an oxidizing agent because each Cl atom is reduced from an oxidation number of $+1$ to -1. Also, I^- is a reducing agent because each I atom is oxidized from an oxidation number of -1 to 0.

$$OCl^- + 2e^- \rightarrow Cl^- \qquad 2I^- \rightarrow I_2 + 2e^-$$

Name _____ Class _____ Date _____

Add one drop of each solution to the indicated space. Add HCl if no reaction occurs. Then write half-reactions and a redox equation, and identify the oxidizing agent and the reducing agent for each. If no reaction occurs, write "NVR."

	$MnO_4^- \rightarrow Mn^{2+}$ $KMnO_4$	$Cr_2O_7^{2-} \rightarrow Cr^{3+}$ $K_2Cr_2O_7$	$I_2 \rightarrow I^-$ $KI + Starch + NaOCl$	$Fe^{3+} \rightarrow Fe^{2+}$ $FeCl_3$
$NaHSO_3$ $HSO_3^- \rightarrow SO_4^{2-}$				
H_2O_2 $H_2O_2 \rightarrow O_2$				
$Na_2S_2O_3$ $S_2O_3^{2-} \rightarrow SO_4^{2-}$				
$NaNO_2$ $NO_2^- \rightarrow NO(g) + NO_3^-$				

What gas produces the bubbles you saw? In which mixtures did you see bubbles?

_____

Describe what happens with each mixing. Make a table of your results.

33 SMALL-SCALE VOLTAIC CELLS

Small-Scale Experiment for text section 23.1

OBJECTIVES

- **Build** and **test** simple voltaic cells.
- **Measure** and **compare** the voltages of commercial cells with the ones you build.
- **Describe** the chemistry of voltaic cells by writing half-reactions.
- **Construct** an electrochemical series from experimental data.

INTRODUCTION

Americans own some 900 million battery-operated devices and spend 2.5 billion dollars a year feeding them batteries. Batteries (voltaic dry cells) are simple devices that transform chemical energy into electrical energy. They operate on the principle of oxidation–reduction chemistry. One chemical inside the battery is a reducing agent and gives up electrons. Another chemical is an oxidizing agent and accepts the electrons given up by the former. The flow of electrons from one chemical to another constitutes an electric current. The device is designed to tap the electric current that flows from reducing agent to oxidizing agent. As the chemical reaction progresses, less and less current is produced. Eventually the current diminishes to the extent that the battery is essentially "dead." At this point we usually throw it away and replace it with a new one.

Which materials make the best batteries? In previous labs you discovered that some metals lose electrons more readily than others. The metal cations that are formed as a result do not gain electrons as readily as do metal cations formed from less reactive metals.

The following list of half-reactions shows the reduction of metal ions to metal atoms. The reverse of each half-reaction is the oxidation half-reaction of the metal. Any metal on the list will react only with a metal ion that is below it in the list. For example, magnesium metal, Mg(s), will react with all of the other metal ions in the list. Iron, Fe(s), will react only with Cu^{2+} and Ag^+. Silver, Ag(s), will not react with any of the metal ions in the list.

$$Mg^{2+} + 2e^- \rightarrow Mg(s)$$
$$Zn^{2+} + 2e^- \rightarrow Zn(s)$$
$$Fe^{3+} + 3e^- \rightarrow Fe(s)$$
$$Cu^{2+} + 2e^- \rightarrow Cu(s)$$
$$Ag^+ + e^- \rightarrow Ag(s)$$

PURPOSE

In this lab you will build some small-scale batteries (voltaic cells) from metals and solutions of metal ions. You will use a volt meter to measure and compare the voltages they produce. You will relate this information to the redox chemistry involved and to the activity series you developed in Small-Scale Experiment 31.

SAFETY

- Wear your safety glasses.
- Use full small-scale pipets only for the carefully controlled delivery of liquids.

MATERIALS

Small-scale pipets of the following solutions:

magnesium sulfate ($MgSO_4$)   zinc chloride ($ZnCl_2$)
sodium nitrate ($NaNO_3$)

silver nitrate ($AgNO_3$)
copper(II) sulfate ($CuSO_4$)
lead(II) nitrate ($Pb(NO_3)_2$)

Solids:
silver (Ag)   lead (Pb)
copper (Cu)   zinc (Zn)
magnesium (Mg)

EQUIPMENT

small-scale reaction surface   volt meter
9-centimeter filter paper   various commercial batteries
scissors   (dry cells)

EXPERIMENTAL PAGE

1. Measure the voltage of these commercial cells: standard carbon, heavy duty, alkaline, rechargeable. (A positive meter reading means the electrons flow into the meter at the connector labeled "−".) Reverse the leads and measure the voltage again. Record your results in Table 33.1.

2. Test copper and zinc in the spaces below. Record your results in Table 33.2.

   a. Mix 2 drops of each of the indicated solutions with one piece of each metal.

	2 drops $CuSO_4$	2 drops $ZnCl_2$	
1 piece Zn			1 piece Cu

   b. Cut and place a rectangular piece of filter paper on the template below, and add 3 drops of each solution so the center solution barely overlaps the other two solutions. Then add one piece of each metal and measure the positive (+) voltage of the cell you just made. Reverse the leads and measure it again. Record your results in Table 33.2.

$CuSO_4$	$NaNO_3$	$ZnCl_2$
Cu(s)		Zn(s)

3. Cut a piece of filter paper as shown below, and add a few drops of each solution so that each "arm" is wet. The $NaNO_3$ solution should touch the other solutions. Place a piece of the indicated metal on each arm and measure the voltages of each lead (Pb) cell with the black, negative (−) connector on "Pb." Press firmly. Record the voltages in Table 33.3.

Place this side of the Experimental Page facedown. Use the other side under your small-scale reaction surface.

Name _____ Class _____ Date _____

EXPERIMENTAL DATA

Record your results in Tables 33.1–33.3 or tables like them in your notebook.

Table 33.1   Commercial Dry Cell Voltages

Name of commercial cell	Voltage	Voltage(with leads reversed)
standard carbon	_____	_____
heavy duty	_____	_____
alkaline	_____	_____
rechargeable	_____	_____

Table 33.2   Copper-Zinc Cell

a. $CuSO_4$ + Zn(s)	$ZnCl_2$ + Cu(s)	b. Voltage of Cu–Zn cell

Table 33.3   Lead Cells

Ag	Cu	Mg	Zn	Pb

Electrons flow
away from:

_____ _____ _____ _____

CLEANING UP

Avoid contamination by cleaning up in a way that protects you and your environment. Carefully clean and dry the pieces of metal and place them in the proper recycling containers. Clean the reaction surface by absorbing the contents onto a paper towel, wipe it with a damp paper towel, and dry it. Dispose of the paper towels in the waste bin. Wash your hands thoroughly with soap and water.

QUESTIONS FOR ANALYSIS

Use what you learned in this lab to answer the following questions.

1. When measuring voltages, what happens when you reverse the red, positive (+) and black, negative (−) leads of the volt meter?

   _____

2. When the meter reads a positive voltage, into which connector do the electrons flow?

   _____

3. Which reaction occurs in Step 2a? Write half-reactions for the reaction.

   _____

4. Based on the sign of the voltage, which metal loses electrons, Cu or Zn? Explain.

   _____

   _____

5. Write the half-reactions for the Cu–Zn cell you constructed in Step **2b**. How do these compare to those you wrote for Step **2a**?

   _____

6. Construct a set of reduction potentials by writing *reduction* half-reactions for all five metals, including lead, from Step **3**. Assign 0.00 volts to Pb, and list the half-reactions in order of increasing voltages (most negative value first).

7. Compare your ordered list of half-reactions to the activity series you developed in Small-Scale Experiment 31. What conclusions can you draw?

   _____

8. Draw a simple cross-sectional diagram of the Zn–Cu cell you made showing the direction of electron flow. Mark the cathode, the anode, and the salt bridge.

9. The table of reduction potentials you constructed above can be used to predict the voltages of a cell made from any two metals on the table. Simply find the difference between the two voltages in question. For example, the voltage of an Ag–Zn cell will probably be about 1.37 volts ($0.84 - -0.53 = 1.37$) Use your reduction potential table above to predict the voltages of the following cells: Ag–Cu, Ag–Zn, Ag–Mg, Cu–Zn, Cu–Mg, Zn–Mg.

NOW IT'S YOUR TURN!

1. Design an experiment to measure the cell voltages of each cell for which you predicted values in Question 9, and compare your results with your predicted values.

2. Make a good guess as to what the metals are in such common metal objects as nickels, dimes, food cans, soda cans, nails, washers, galvanized nails, etc. Test each of your predictions by replacing one of the metal electrodes in Step 3 of the experiment with the common metal object in question. What common metal is each object made from? Are your results conclusive? Suggest an explanation.

3. Go shopping and record the prices of various types of the same sizes of commercial voltaic cells (batteries). The following table compares the lifetimes of various commercial batteries. Use your data and the table to decide which type of battery is the most cost-effective.

Type of cell	Expected lifetime (hours)*	Price
General purpose (zinc-carbon)	1–7	_____
Heavy duty (zinc-chloride)	1.5–15	_____
Alkaline	5–27	_____
Rechargeable (nickel-cadmium)**	2–7	_____

*The expected lifetime varies with the size of the battery, the device in which it is used, and whether it is used continuously or intermittently.
**Can be recharged up to 1,000 times with a recharger.

34 TITRATION OF BLEACH

Small-Scale Experiment for text section 24.2

OBJECTIVE

- **Measure** and **record** the amount of sodium hypochlorite in household bleach.

INTRODUCTION

Sodium hypochlorite, NaOCl, is a common chemical that has many household applications. Sodium hypochlorite is the active ingredient in household bleach, liquid drain openers, powdered cleansers, and automatic dish washing liquids. The hypochlorite ion, OCl^-, is useful in these cleaners because it is a powerful oxidizing agent. Hypochlorite ion as an oxidizing agent is able to whiten, brighten, or otherwise remove the color from all sorts of materials. For example, manufacturers of paper and textiles often use some sort of bleach to whiten their products and prepare them to be dyed.

The hypochlorite ion is also useful as a disinfectant. Hypochlorous acid, HOCl, is very toxic to bacteria. A very small concentration of about one part per million (1 ppm) is required to kill bacteria. The small OCl^- ion easily penetrates the cell of a bacterium. Once inside, its strong oxidizing effect destroys the bacterium protein.

Swimming pools are typically treated with hypochlorite ion to disinfect the water and keep it sanitary. One pool sanitizer is calcium hypochlorite, $Ca(OCl)_2$, which introduces hypochlorite ion directly into the water. Larger pools commonly contain chlorine gas, which reacts with water to produce hypochlorous acid:

$$Cl_2(g) + H_2O \rightarrow HOCl + H^+ + Cl^-$$

Another kind of bleach is an "oxygen bleach." Examples of oxygen bleaches are hydrogen peroxide, H_2O_2, and sodium perborate, Na_3BO_4. Many laundry detergents advertise that they contain "color safe" bleach, meaning that the active ingredient is sodium perborate. Sodium perborate, an oxygen bleach, is much milder than sodium hypochlorite, the active ingredient in "chlorine bleach." In fact, sodium hypochlorite is so powerful it can fray or discolor fabric, and dissolve stitching. Even so, consumer tests have shown repeatedly that chlorine bleach (containing sodium hypochlorite) is superior to oxygen bleaches (containing hydrogen peroxide or sodium perborate) at removing stains and brightening fabrics.

The use of all products that contain sodium hypochlorite can be dangerous. Sodium hypochlorite reacts with hydrochloric acid to produce toxic chlorine gas:

$$NaOCl + 2HCl \rightarrow NaCl + H_2O + Cl_2(g)$$

For this reason one should avoid mixing household bleach or any other product containing sodium hypochlorite with other household products such as toilet-bowl cleaners that contain acid. Warning labels on bottles of household bleach are very clear about this:

Warning! Do not mix with other chemicals, such as toilet-bowl cleaners, rust removers, acid or ammonia containing products. To do so will release hazardous gases.

PURPOSE

In this lab you will use sodium thiosulfate, $Na_2S_2O_3$, to determine the amount of sodium hypochlorite, NaOCl, in household bleach. Your method will be iodometric titration. That is, you will add starch, ethanoic acid (CH_3COOH), and iodide ion (KI) to a dilute solution of bleach (NaOCl). This will cause a reaction producing iodine. The starch acts as an indicator, turning the mixture blue-black in color. You will then titrate the iodine with thiosulfate. In the titration, you will measure the amount of sodium thiosulfate it takes to change the mixture from blue-black to colorless at the end point. The measured amount of $Na_2S_2O_3$ is directly proportional to the amount of NaOCl in the bleach.

You will begin by examining the chemistry of the titration and then apply it to the analysis of a bleach sample. Finally, you will design and carry out experiments to find out how much sodium hypochlorite there is in other consumer products.

SAFETY 👓

- Wear your safety glasses.
- Use full small-scale pipets only for the carefully controlled delivery of liquids.

MATERIALS

Small-scale pipets of the following solutions:
sodium thiosulfate ($Na_2S_2O_3$)	ethanoic acid (CH_3COOH)
potassium iodide (KI)	starch
diluted household bleach	

sodium hypochlorite (NaOCl)

EQUIPMENT

small-scale reaction surface
plastic cup
12-well strip

EXPERIMENTAL PROCEDURE

Part A. Some Chemistry of NaOCl

1. Place one drop of NaOCl on a small-scale reaction surface and add the solutions mentioned in the following steps. Stir each mixture and record your results in Table 34.1.

a. Add 1 drop of KI and 1 drop of CH_3COOH to the drop of NaOCl in Step 1. In acid solution, hypochlorite ion oxidizes iodide ion to iodine:

$$OCl^- + 2I^- + 2H^+ \rightarrow Cl^- + H_2O + I_2$$

b. Add a few more drops of KI to the mixture. Excess iodide ion reacts with iodine to form triiodide ion: $I^- + I_2 \rightarrow I_3^-$

c. Now add a drop of starch. Starch reacts with triiodide ion to form a starch-iodine complex: $I_3^- + starch \rightarrow$ starch-iodine complex.

d. Now add several drops of $Na_2S_2O_3$ until the reaction mixture turns colorless. Thiosulfate ion reduces triiodide to iodide ion:

$$I_3^- + 2S_2O_3^{2-} \rightarrow 3I^- + S_4O_6^{2-}$$

Part B. Titration of Sodium Hypochlorite in Bleach with Sodium Thiosulfate

2. Carry out the following procedure for the titration of bleach.

a. Calibrate a $Na_2S_2O_3$ pipet. (Count the number of drops to fill a well.)

b. Calibrate a NaOCl (bleach) pipet. (Count the number of drops to fill a well.)

c. Using the same pipet, add the same number of drops of NaOCl it took to fill a well to a clean, dry cup.

d. Add in order: 3 drops starch, 25 drops KI, and 20 drops CH_3COOH.

e. Titrate the NaOCl with $Na_2S_2O_3$ to a colorless end point. (Count the number of drops of $Na_2S_2O_3$ it takes to change the mixture from black to colorless.)

f. Repeat the experiment until your results are consistent.

Name _____ Class _____ Date _____

EXPERIMENTAL DATA

Record your results in Tables 34.1 and 34.2 or tables like them in your notebook.

Table 34.1   Chemistry of NaOCl

	NaOCl	$KI + CH_3COOH$	Excess KI	Starch	$Na_2S_2O_3$
Color					

Table 34.2   Titration of Bleach

	Drops $Na_2S_2O_3$ to fill	Drops NaOCl to fill	Drops NaOCl in cup	Drops $Na_2S_2O_3$ to end point	NaOCl conc. mol/L
NaOCl Sample 1					
2					
3					

Calculate the concentration in mol NaOCl/L of sodium hypochlorite in the bleach samples you titrated. Record your results in Table 34.2. To do the calculation, you will need the following pieces of information:

a. The drops of $Na_2S_2O_3$ used to obtain a colorless end point in the titration.

b. The drops of NaOCl added to the cup.

c. The drops of NaOCl needed to fill a well in drops/well.

d. The drops of $Na_2S_2O_3$ needed to fill a well in drops/well.

e. The concentration of $Na_2S_2O_3 = 0.1\ M$.

f. The overall stoichiometry = 1 mol NaOCl/2 mol $Na_2S_2O_3$.

$$\frac{x \text{ mol NaOCl}}{\text{L NaOCl}} = \frac{a}{b} \times \frac{c}{d} \times e \times f$$

To be sure you understand the calculation, substitute each quantity (number and unit) into the equation and cancel the units. For subsequent calculations, simplify the equation by combining terms that are always constant. For example, in this experiment, the number of drops of NaOCl added to the cup is equal to the number of drops of NaOCl it took to fill a well, so **b** = **c** and they cancel.

$$xM \text{ NaOCl} = \frac{a}{1} \times \frac{1}{d} \times e \times f = \frac{aef}{d}$$

CLEANING UP

Avoid contamination by cleaning up in a way that protects you and your environment. Carefully clean the reaction surface by absorbing the contents onto a dry paper towel, wipe it with a damp paper towel, and dry it. Rinse out the cup, wipe it with a damp paper towel, and dry it. Dispose of the towels in the waste bin. Wash your hands thoroughly with soap and water.

QUESTIONS FOR ANALYSIS

Use what you learned in this lab to answer the following questions.

1. What happens when you add NaOCl to KI and CH_3COOH? What is the colored product? Write the net ionic equation (see Experimental Procedure).

   _____

2. A few more drops of KI produces what change? Write the net ionic equation for the reaction of excess potassium iodide with iodine (see Experimental Page).

   _____

3. What happens when you add starch? Write the equation for the reaction between triiodide and starch.

   _____

4. What color is the final mixture after you add sodium thiosulfate? Write the net ionic equation for the reaction between triiodide and sodium thiosulfate.

   _____

5. Explain how starch acts as an indicator for the presence or absence of triiodide.

   _____

6. Calculate the percent of NaOCl in the bleach, using the number of moles of NaOCl per liter that you calculated from your Experimental Data.

   $$\% \text{ NaOCl} = \frac{g \text{ NaOCl}}{100 \text{ g soln}} = \frac{\mathbf{0.13} \text{ moles NaOCl}}{\text{L soln}} \times \frac{74.5 \text{ g NaOCl}}{\text{mol NaOCl}} \times \frac{1 \text{ L soln}}{1000 \text{ g soln}} \times 100 = \mathbf{0.97\%}$$

7. Multiply the percent of NaOCl in bleach from Question 6 by 5 (the bleach sample you titrated was diluted by a factor of 5), and compare your result to the percent of NaOCl listed on the bleach bottle's label by calculating the percent error and suggesting possible sources of error.

$$\% \text{ error} = \frac{5 \times \text{your result} - \% \text{ on label}}{\% \text{ on label}} \times 100$$

_____

_____

_____

_____

NOW IT'S YOUR TURN!

1. Design and carry out some weight titration experiments, using your small-scale balance or other balance to determine the molar concentration of NaOCl in bleach. Compare your results to your volumetric titrations.

_____

_____

_____

_____

2. The labels of many household products say they contain sodium hypochlorite. Dish-washing-machine liquids often contain NaOCl. Design and carry out some experiments to determine the molar concentration of NaOCl in some household dish-washing-machine liquids.

3. Design some experiments to show that sodium hypochlorite is not "color-safe."

_____

_____

35 FORMATION OF COMPLEX IONS WITH AMMONIA

Small-Scale Experiment for text section 24.3

OBJECTIVES

- **Observe** the formation of complex ions when various cations react with ammonia.
- **Identify** metal cations that form complex ions with ammonia.
- **Describe** the formation of complex ions by writing net ionic equations.

INTRODUCTION

You have seen in previous labs that ammonia, NH_3, is a base because it reacts with water to produce hydroxide ions in solution:

$$NH_3 + H_2O \rightleftharpoons NH_4^+ + OH^-$$

Ammonia also reacts with a variety of metal cations in aqueous solution to form complex ions. A *complex* ion is an ion containing one or more molecules bonded to a central metal ion. For example, you are already familiar with the royal blue color that results from mixing a copper ion (Cu^{2+}) with ammonia. This reaction produces the highly colored, distinctive complex ion, $Cu(NH_3)_4^{2+}$, called the tetrammonium copper(II) ion.

$$Cu^{2+} + 4NH_3 \rightleftharpoons Cu(NH_3)_4^{2+}$$
$$\text{royal blue}$$

This reaction is an example of a Lewis acid–base reaction. Copper(II) acts as a Lewis acid because it accepts an electron pair from ammonia. Ammonia is a Lewis base, because it donates an electron pair. The bond between ammonia and copper(II) is a coordinate covalent bond because both electrons come from the ammonia.

While many complex ions are highly colored species, others show only subtle colors or none at all. Hence, color is a limited tool in detecting complex ion formation. In this lab you will detect the formation of colorless complex ions by probing the solubility of certain precipitates in the presence of excess ammonia. Dissolution of the precipitate suggests the formation of a complex ion with ammonia. For example, silver ion will react with carbonate ion to produce silver carbonate:

$$2Ag^+ + CO_3^{2-} \rightleftharpoons Ag_2CO_3(s)$$

Silver ion also reacts with ammonia to produce a colorless complex ion:

$$Ag^+ + 2NH_3 \rightleftharpoons Ag(NH_3)_2^+$$

When you add ammonia to an aqueous mixture of solid silver carbonate, you will find that the precipitate dissolves. Both of the above equilibria compete for the silver ion, and the formation of the complex ion predominates. That is, the complex-ion reaction lies farther to the right than does the precipitation reaction. Le Châtelier's principle predicts that the first reaction will shift to the left as the second reaction consumes silver ions. Thus, the precipitate will disappear.

PURPOSE

In this lab you will precipitate various metal cations as carbonates. You will then use excess ammonia ion as a probe to determine which of these precipitates dissolve. You can conclude that dissolution of a carbonate precipitate in the presence of excess ammonia is evidence for the formation of a complex ion.

SAFETY

- Wear your safety glasses.
- Use full small-scale pipets only for the carefully controlled delivery of liquids.

MATERIALS

Small-scale pipets of the following aqueous solutions:

sodium hydrogen carbonate (NaHCO$_3$)   3 M ammonia (NH$_3$)
aluminum chloride (AlCl$_3$)   sodium chloride (NaCl)
zinc chloride (ZnCl$_2$)   calcium chloride (CaCl$_2$)
iron(III) chloride (FeCl$_3$)   magnesium sulfate (MgSO$_4$)
tin(IV) chloride (SnCl$_4$)

copper(II) sulfate (CuSO$_4$)
silver nitrate (AgNO$_3$)
lead(II) nitrate (Pb(NO$_3$)$_2$)

EQUIPMENT

small-scale reaction surface
empty pipet for stirring

EXPERIMENTAL PAGE

On each **X** below, mix 1 drop of $NaHCO_3$ with 2 drops of each indicated solution. Stir by blowing air through an empty pipet. Then add several drops of NH_3 and stir.

	1 drop $NaHCO_3$		1 drop $NaHCO_3$
2 drops each		2 drops each	
a. $CuSO_4$ (Cu^{2+})	X	**f.** $AgNO_3$ (Ag^+)	X
b. $AlCl_3$ (Al^{3+})	X	**g.** $NaCl$ (Na^+)	X
c. $FeCl_3$ (Fe^{3+})	X	**h.** $SnCl_4$ (Sn^{4+})	X
d. $MgSO_4$ (Mg^{2+})	X	**i.** $Pb(NO_3)_2$ (Pb^{2+})	X
e. $CaCl_2$ (Ca^{2+})	X	**j.** $ZnCl_2$ (Zn^{2+})	X

Place this side of the Experimental Page facedown. Use the other side under your small-scale reaction surface.

Name _____ Class _____ Date _____

EXPERIMENTAL DATA

Record your results in Table 35.1 or a table like it in your notebook.

Table 35.1   Complex Ions with Ammonia

a. $CuSO_4$ (Cu^{2+})		**f.** $AgNO_3$ (Ag^+)	
b. $AlCl_3$ (Al^{3+})		**g.** $NaCl$ (Na^+)	
c. $FeCl_3$ (Fe^{3+})		**h.** $SnCl_4$ (Sn^{4+})	
d. $MgSO_4$ (Mg^{2+})		**i.** $Pb(NO_3)_2$ (Pb^{2+})	
e. $CaCl_2$ (Ca^{2+})		**j.** $ZnCl_2$ (Zn^{2+})	

CLEANING UP

Avoid contamination by cleaning up in a way that protects you and your environment. Carefully clean the reaction surface by absorbing the contents onto a paper towel, wipe it with a damp paper towel, and dry it. Dispose of the paper towels in the waste bin. Wash your hands thoroughly with soap and water.

QUESTIONS FOR ANALYSIS

Use what you learned in this lab to answer the following questions.

1. Write net ionic equations for each precipitation reaction you observed.

   _____   _____

   _____   _____

   _____   _____

   _____   _____

2. Precipitates of cations that dissolve upon addition of excess ammonia form complex ions with ammonia. Which cations form complex ions with ammonia? Ask your instructor for the formulas of each complex ion.

_____

3. Write net ionic equations to describe the formation of each complex ion. Identify each Lewis acid and Lewis base.

4. What are the colors of the complex ions?

_____

NOW IT'S YOUR TURN!

1. Devise an experiment to determine the cations that form complex ions with ammonia by employing a different precipitate. How do your results compare with this lab? Try forming the initial precipitates with sodium phosphate and sodium hydroxide.

2. Devise an experiment to determine the cations that form complex ions with ammonia using an excess of cation and only a small amount of ammonia as a source of hydroxide to bring down the original precipitates as hydroxides. For example, add 1 drop of ammonia, NH_3, to two drops of copper(II) sulfate, $CuSO_4$. Because ammonia is a weak base it is a source of hydroxide ions:

$$NH_3 + H_2O \rightleftharpoons NH_4^+ + OH^-$$

A small amount of ammonia added to an excess of copper ions will produce a light blue copper(II) hydroxide precipitate:

$$Cu^{2+} + 2OH^- \rightarrow Cu(OH)_2(s)$$

Now add several more drops of ammonia and stir. Excess ammonia will cause copper ions to react to form the royal blue complex ion, $Cu(NH_3)_4^{2+}$:

$$Cu^{2+} + 4NH_3 \rightleftharpoons Cu(NH_3)_4^{2+} \text{ (royal blue solution)}$$

Try adding a little ammonia to an excess of the other cations in this experiment. Then add excess ammonia and see what happens. How do your results compare to the original experiments?

_____

_____

36 MOLECULAR STRUCTURE OF HYDROCARBONS

Small-Scale Experiment for text sections 25.1 and 25.2

OBJECTIVES

- **Construct** models of hydrocarbon molecules.
- **Compare** the structures of hydrocarbons with their chemical formulas.
- **Compare** the structures of alkanes, alkenes, and alkynes.

INTRODUCTION

Chemical formulas give you information about the compositions of substances as well as their structures. Organic chemistry uses many different kinds of formulas and models to describe the compositions and structures of molecules.

A *molecular formula* gives limited information about a compound. Only the actual number and kinds of atoms present in a molecule of a compound are shown. A *structural formula* is more useful for studying organic compounds because it shows the arrangement of each atom and each bond in a molecule. Different structural arrangements of the same molecular formula are called isomers. An *expanded structural formula* actually shows each atom and each bond. A *condensed structural formula* is a shorthand method for writing a structural formula. A *line-angle formula* for a hydrocarbon uses straight lines to represent each carbon-carbon bond. Carbon atoms are understood to be at the ends of each line. Hydrogen atoms are not shown at all. Instead, it is understood that there are enough hydrogen atoms for each carbon atom to have 4 bonds. A *ball-and-stick diagram* of a molecule shows the three-dimensional arrangement of each atom and each bond. Finally, a *space-filling model* gives a clearer picture of the relative sizes of atoms and the distances between them.

	Molecular and line-angle formula	Expanded and condensed structural formulas	Ball-and-stock diagram	Space-filling model
Butane	C_4H_{10}	H—C—C—C—C—H with H atoms; $CH_3CH_2CH_2CH_3$		
2-methylpropane	C_4H_{10}	H—C—C—C—H structure; CH_3CHCH_3 with CH_3		

PURPOSE

In this lab you will make models of various hydrocarbons to study their three-dimensional structures. You will use pipe cleaners, pop beads, and polystyrene spheres to make your models. The pipe cleaners will represent the bonds; the polystyrene spheres will represent the carbon atoms; and the pop beads will represent the hydrogen atoms. Black pipe cleaners will represent carbon-carbon bonds and white pipe cleaners will represent carbon-hydrogen bonds. You will bend the pipe cleaners into angles to better represent the three-dimensional geometry of molecules.

SAFETY

- Behave in a way that is consistent with a safe laboratory.

EQUIPMENT

6 one-inch polystyrene spheres
12 pop beads
3 black and 3 white pipe cleaners
scissors
ruler

EXPERIMENTAL PROCEDURE

Make a model of each hydrocarbon indicated on Table 36.1, and use the information to fill in Table 36.1 or a table like it.

1. Construct a ball-and-stick model of methane, CH_4.

   a. Place four 2-cm pieces of white pipe cleaner in a polystyrene sphere, arranging them so they form a tetrahedron with angles slightly larger than right angles. (The ideal bond angles in methane are all 109.5°.)

   b. Place a pop bead on the end of each of the 4 pipe cleaners.

2. Construct a ball-and-stick model of ethane, CH_3CH_3.

   a. Connect 2 polystyrene spheres with a 5-cm piece of black pipe cleaner.

   b. Place three 2-cm pieces of white pipe cleaner in each polystyrene sphere, arranging them so they form a tetrahedron with angles slightly larger than right angles. (The ideal bond angles in ethane are all 109.5°.)

   c. Place a pop bead on the end of each of the 6 pipe cleaners.

3. Construct a ball-and-stick model of propane, $CH_3CH_2CH_3$.

   a. Connect 3 polystyrene spheres with two 5-cm pieces of black pipe cleaner, adjusting the angle formed by the pipe cleaners to be slightly greater than a right angle.

   b. Place two 2-cm pieces of white pipe cleaner in the center sphere and three in each of the end spheres. Adjust all the angles so they are slightly greater than right angles.

   c. Place a pop bead on the end of each of the 8 pipe cleaners.

4. Use the same techniques to construct models of the following hydrocarbons. Be sure each carbon has 4 bonds.

   a. butane, $CH_3CH_2CH_2CH_3$ (See p. 259.)

   b. 2-methylbutane (See p. 259.)

   c. pentane, $CH_3CH_2CH_2CH_2CH_3$

5. Ethene is an alkene. All 6 atoms lie in the same plane with bond angles of 120°.

   a. Construct a model of ethene, $CH_2 = CH_2$.

   b. Construct a model of propene, $CH_3CH = CH_2$.

6. Ethyne is an alkyne. All 4 atoms lie in a straight line.

   a. Construct a model of ethyne, $CH \equiv CH$.

   b. Construct a model of propyne, $CH_3C \equiv CH$.

EXPERIMENTAL DATA

Record your results in Table 36.1 or a table like it in your notebook.

Table 36.1   Models of Hydrocarbons

Name	Molecular Formula	Structural Formula	Ball-and-Stick Diagram	Bond Angles
1. methane				
2. ethane				
3. propane				
4a. butane				
b. 2-methylbutane				
c. pentane				
5a. ethene				
b. propene				
6a. ethyne				
b. propyne				

CLEANING UP

When you finish, take apart your models, straighten out each piece of pipe cleaner, and put them away.

QUESTIONS FOR ANALYSIS

Use what you learned in this lab to answer the following questions.

1. What information does a molecular formula give? Give an example.

   _____

2. What information does a structural formula give? Give an example.

   _____

   _____

3. What's the difference between an expanded structural formula and a condensed structural formula?

   _____

   _____

4. What's the difference between a ball-and-stick model and a space-filling model? Which is more representative of the true structure of a molecule?

   _____

   _____

5. The atoms around a carbon-carbon single bond exhibit what bond angles?

   _____

6. The atoms around a carbon-carbon double bond exhibit what bond angles?

   _____

7. The atoms around a carbon-carbon triple bond exhibit what bond angles?

   _____

NOW IT'S YOUR TURN!

1. Construct models of the following cyclic hydrocarbons that contain hydrocarbon rings.

   a. cyclopropane (Hint: Attach the black ends of your propane model.)

   b. cyclobutane

2. Longer chain alkenes have *cis* and *trans* geometric isomers (text Section 25.3). Construct models of 1-butene $(CH_2 = CHCH_2CH_3)$ and 2-butene $(CH_3CH = CHCH_3)$. Which has geometric isomers? Construct models of each geometric isomer.

_____

3. Construct models of 1-butyne, $C \equiv CCH_2CH_3$, and 2-butyne, $CH_3C \equiv CCH_3$. Use them to determine if either of these alkynes have geometric isomers.

_____

_____

_____

4. Benzene, C_6H_6, is an aromatic hydrocarbon (text Section 25.4). All 12 of its atoms lie in the same plane. Its 6 carbon atoms lie in a flat ring. Construct a model of benzene.

5. Construct a model of methane, CH_4, without using spheres as atoms. Compare it to your ball-and-stick model.

    a. Fold two 4-cm pieces of white pipe cleaner in half, making a bend at each center.

    b. Interlock the pipe cleaners and pinch them together at the bends.

    c. Unfold the 4 ends so they make angles slightly larger than right angles.

6. Construct a line-angle model of ethane, CH_3CH_3, without using spheres as atoms. Compare it to your ball-and-stick model.

    a. Make another model of methane.

    b. Cut a 5-cm piece of black pipe cleaner and bend a small hook at each end.

    c. Attach a methane molecule to each end of the black pipe cleaner by pinching a hook around each methane's center. (How many bonds does each carbon have in your model?)

    d. Eliminate a hydrogen from each end by twisting together any two of the white pipe cleaners.

    e. Arrange all the angles so they are slightly larger than right angles.

7. Construct a model of propane, $CH_3CH_2CH_3$.

    a. Cut a 10-cm piece of black pipe cleaner and fold it in half.

    b. Fold a 4-cm piece of white pipe cleaner in half, and pinch together the black and white pipe cleaners at their folds.

    c. Attach a methane molecule to each end, as with ethane, and twist together two hydrogens at each end.

    d. Make all the angles slightly larger than right angles.

37 VITAMIN C IN TABLETS

Small-Scale Experiment for text section 26.3

OBJECTIVES

- **Determine** the vitamin C content of commercial vitamin C tablets by iodometric titration.
- **Observe** the oxidation of vitamin C in aqueous solution.

INTRODUCTION

Vitamins are chemical compounds that are essential to human health. These compounds regulate biochemical reactions that take place within living cells. The human body requires vitamins only in tiny amounts. For a compound to be classified as a vitamin, its absence in the diet must cause a specific disease that is cured when the vitamin is resupplied. Vitamin C deficiency, for example, causes scurvy, a disease common to seamen until the latter part of the eighteenth century. Scurvy is cured by increasing the intake of vitamin C.

PURPOSE

In this lab you will use an iodometric titration to measure the amount of vitamin C in various commercially available vitamin supplements. This method takes advantage of the fact that vitamin C is a water-soluble organic compound that is easily oxidized and is therefore a good reducing agent. Iodine oxidizes vitamin C according to the following equation:

$$+ I_2 \rightarrow 2H^+ + 2I^- +$$

$C_6H_8O_6$
Vitamin C
(Ascorbic acid)

$C_6H_6O_6$
Oxidized form of vitamin C
(Dehydroascorbic acid)

Because aqueous iodine solutions are unstable and inconvenient to work with, you will titrate vitamin C samples in this lab with potassium iodate, KIO_3, in the presence of an acidic iodide solution. The iodate ion oxidizes iodide to iodine:

$$IO_3^- + 5I^- + 6H^+ \rightleftharpoons 3I_2 + 3H_2O$$

Notice that an equilibrium is established between reactants and products. To insure that the reaction goes to completion (far to the right), it is necessary to use excess iodide and to make the solution acidic.

The iodine formed in this reaction immediately oxidizes the vitamin C according to the previous equation. Once all the vitamin C is oxidized, there will be an excess of I_2 that will react with starch to form the distinctive blue-black complex. This change serves as a good end point.

SAFETY

- Wear your safety glasses.
- Use full small-scale pipets only for the carefully controlled delivery of liquids.

MATERIALS

Small-scale pipets of the following solutions:

potassium iodide (KI)
starch

$0.1M$ potassium iodate (KIO_3)

vitamin C (ascorbic acid)
various vitamin C tablets (100 mg)

hydrochloric acid (HCl)

EQUIPMENT

plastic cup, small-scale reaction surface, balance

EXPERIMENTAL PROCEDURE

Part A. The Chemistry of the Titration

1. Place 2 drops of KIO_3 on a small-scale reaction surface, and add the following solutions. Stir each mixture and record your results in Table 37.1.

   a. Add 2 drops of KI and 2 drops of HCl. In acid solution, iodate ion oxidizes iodide ion to iodine: $IO_3^- + 5I^- + 6H^+ \rightleftharpoons 3I_2 + 3H_2O$

   b. Add a few more drops of KI to the above mixture. Excess iodide ion reacts with iodine to form triiodide ion: $I^- + I_2 \rightarrow I_3^-$

   c. Now add 1 drop of starch. Starch reacts with triiodide ion to form a starch iodine complex: I_3^- + starch $\rightarrow$ starch-iodine complex

   d. Now add vitamin C, stirring until the black color disappears. Vitamin C reduces iodine to iodide ion: $C_6H_8O_6 + I_2 \rightarrow 2H^- + 2I^- + C_6H_6O_6$

   e. Finally, add KIO_3 until the black color reappears. At this point, all the vitamin C has reacted and the excess iodate reacts to form iodine, which gives the black end point in the presence of starch.

Part B. Titration of Vitamin C in Tablets

2. Crush a vitamin C tablet on a piece of paper, and transfer *all* of it to a clean, dry cup.

3. Add 10 drops KI, 2 drops HCl, and 3 drops starch.

4. Tare or weigh a full KIO_3 pipet.

   a. Place a full KIO_3 pipet in a clean dry small-scale balance pan.

   b. Adjust the beam until the small-scale pointer indicates the zero point.

5. Titrate the vitamin C with KIO_3 to a jet black end point.

6. Determine the weight loss of the KIO_3. Record your findings in Table 37.2.

   a. Replace the pipet on the small-scale balance.

   b. Add weights to zero the small-scale balance again. The sum of the added weights is the weight loss of the KIO_3.

7. Repeat until your results are consistent.

EXPERIMENTAL DATA

Record your results in Tables 37.1 and 37.2 or tables like them in your notebook.

Table 37.1　The Chemistry of the Titration

	KIO_3	KI + HCl	Excess KI	Starch	Vitamin C	KIO_3
Color						

Table 37.2　Titration of Vitamin C in Tablets

	1	2	3	4
Tablet Weight loss of KIO_3 (mg)				
Vitamin C per tablet (mg)				

Calculate the milligrams of vitamin C in each tablet you titrated. Record your results in Table 37.2. To do the calculation you will need the following pieces of information:

a. The weight loss of KIO_3 used in the titration in mg.

b. The density of the KIO_3 solution = 1 mL/1000 mg.

c. The concentration of KIO_3 = 0.1 mmol/mL.

d. Overall stoichiometry = 3 mmol vitamin C/1 mmol of KIO_3.

e. The molecular weight of vitamin C = 176 mg/mmol.

   $$\text{mg Vitamin C} = \mathbf{a} \times \mathbf{b} \times \mathbf{c} \times \mathbf{d} \times \mathbf{e}$$

To be sure you understand the calculation, substitute each quantity (number and units) into the equation and cancel the units. For subsequent calculations, simplify the equation by combining terms that are always constant.

CLEANING UP

Avoid contamination by cleaning up in a way that protects you and your environment. Carefully clean the plastic cup by pouring the liquid contents down the drain and rinsing it thoroughly with water. Dry it with a paper towel. Clean the reaction surface by absorbing the contents onto a paper towel, wipe it with a damp paper towel, and dry it. Dispose of the paper towels in the waste bin. Wash your hands thoroughly with soap and water.

Name _____ Class _____ Date _____

QUESTIONS FOR ANALYSIS

Use what you learned in this lab to answer the following questions.

1. When you mix KI, KIO_3, and HCl, what is produced? How can you tell? Write the net ionic equation.

   _____

2. When you add vitamin C to the black I_2 mixture, why does the color disappear? Write a net ionic equation.

   _____

3. Compare the values for the amount of vitamin C you calculated with the values you find on the product label by calculating the absolute error and the relative error.

   absolute error = |mg measured experimentally − mg on label|

$$\text{relative (\%) error} = \frac{\text{absolute error}}{\text{mg on label}} \times 100$$

4. Why can the density of the KIO_3 solution be taken as 1000 mg/mL?

   _____

NOW IT'S YOUR TURN!

1. Design and carry out an experiment to determine the amount of vitamin C in tablets containing amounts of vitamin C larger than 100 mg. Tell what you do, what your results are, and what they mean.

   _____

   _____

2. Design an experiment to measure the amount of vitamin C in a tablet by using volumetric techniques. Compare your results to those obtained from the weight titration in this lab. (Hint: Dissolve the vitamin C tablet in a known amount of water, and titrate a measured amount of the resulting solution. You will have to calibrate your pipets by using a balance or a well strip.)

3. Dissolve a vitamin C tablet in water, and design an experiment to measure the amount of vitamin C that remains as a function of time. How does temperature affect your results?

38 VITAMIN C IN DRINKS

Small-Scale Experiment for text section 26.3

OBJECTIVE

- **Measure** and **compare** the amounts of vitamin C in various kinds of fruit juices and fruit-drink mixes.

INTRODUCTION

If you have decided to obtain your vitamin C from a well-balanced diet, you may be wondering, "What is the best source of vitamin C, and how much of it do I need to eat or drink?" Orange juice is well-known for its vitamin C content, but many other foods, especially fresh fruits and vegetables, provide substantial amounts of the nutrient. Most noteworthy are other citrus fruits like lemons, tangerines, and grapefruits. Other good sources of vitamin C are asparagus, broccoli, Brussels sprouts, cauliflower, cabbage, cantaloupe, green peppers, parsley, spinach, rutabagas, and turnip greens. However, prolonged cooking of fresh vegetables in water destroys much of the existing vitamin C.

PURPOSE

In this lab you will use the iodometric titration technique you learned in Small-Scale Experiment 37 to determine the vitamin C content of various foods. You will compare the vitamin C content of fresh-squeezed orange juice, frozen orange juice concentrate, and grapefruit juice. You will also measure and compare the vitamin C content of other juices and fruit-drink mixes.

SAFETY 🥽

- Wear your safety glasses.
- Use full small-scale pipets only for the carefully controlled delivery of liquids.
- Consider all foods used in this lab to be contaminated. Do not taste any samples or eat or drink anything in the laboratory.

MATERIALS

Small-scale pipets of the following solutions:

0.01M potassium iodate (KIO_3)   hydrochloric acid (HCl)

potassium iodide (KI)   starch
various samples of fruit
   juices and fruit drinks

EQUIPMENT

plastic cup

EXPERIMENTAL PROCEDURE

1. Weigh approximately 5000 mg of juice. Record the weight in Table 38.1.

   a. Place a nickel (or 2 pennies) of known weight in the balance pan.

   b. Adjust the balance to zero.

   c. Remove the nickel, and add juice until the balance again reads zero.

2. Add 10 drops of KI, 20 drops of HCl, and 5 drops of starch to the juice.

3. Weigh or tare a full KIO_3 pipet.

   a. Place a full KIO_3 pipet in a second clean, dry balance pan.

   b. Adjust the beam until the pointer indicates the zero point.

4. Titrate the juice with KIO_3 to a jet black end point.

5. Determine the weight loss of the KIO_3. Record your results in Table 38.1.

   a. Replace the KIO_3 pipet in the balance.

   b. Add weights to zero the balance. The sum of the added weights is the weight loss of KIO_3.

6. Repeat until your results are consistent.

7. Repeat for several other juice samples as directed by your instructor.

Name _____ Class _____ Date _____

EXPERIMENTAL DATA

Record your results in Table 38.1 or a table like it in your notebook.

Table 38.1 Vitamin C in Drinks

	Wt. of juice (mg)	Wt. loss of KIO_3 (mg)	Vitamin C per 6-oz glass (mg)
Fresh orange juice			
Frozen orange juice			
Fresh grapefruit juice			

Calculate the milligrams of vitamin C in a 6-ounce glass for each sample you titrated. Record your results in Table 38.1. To do the calculation you will need the following pieces of information:

a. The weight loss of the KIO_3 you used in the titration in mg.

b. The weight of the juice you used in the titration in mg.

c. Density of juice = 1000 mg/mL.

d. Density of KIO_3 solution = 1000 mg/mL.

e. Concentration of KIO_3 = 0.01 mmol/mL.

f. Molecular weight of vitamin C = 176 mg/mmol.

g. Overall stoichiometry: 3 mmol vitamin C/1 mmol KIO_3.

h. 29.6 mL/1 oz.

i. 6 oz/1 glass.

$$\frac{x \text{ mg vitamin C}}{1 \text{ glass}} = \frac{a}{b} \times \frac{c}{d} \times e \times f \times g \times h \times i$$

To be sure you understand the calculation, substitute each quantity (number and units) into the equation and cancel the units. For subsequent calculations, simplify the equation by combining terms that are always constant.

CLEANING UP

Avoid contamination by cleaning up in a way that protects you and your environment. Carefully clean the plastic balance pan by pouring the liquid contents down the drain and rinsing it thoroughly with water. Dry it with a paper towel. Dispose of the paper towels in the waste bin. Wash your hands thoroughly with soap and water.

Name _____ Class _____ Date _____

QUESTIONS FOR ANALYSIS

Use your Experimental Data and what you learned in this lab to answer the following questions.

1. Write a net ionic equation for the reaction of iodate ion with iodide ion in the presence of acid. (See Small-Scale Experiment 37.)

   _____

2. Given the two half-reactions for the reaction of Vitamin C with iodine, identify the oxidation and the reduction, and write and balance an equation in acid solution:

   _____ $C_6H_8O_6 \rightarrow C_6H_6O_6 + 2e^-$

   _____ $I_2 + 2e^- \rightarrow 2I^-$

   net ionic: _____

3. The recommended dietary allowance (RDA) is the amount of any vitamin or mineral your daily diet should supply to maintain a general standard of good health. The RDA of vitamin C is 60 milligrams. Calculate how many ounces of each of the various fruit juices you need to consume to receive the RDA of vitamin C.

   $$\text{oz. of juice} = 60 \text{ mg} \times \frac{6 \text{ oz of juice}}{\text{mg vitamin C}}$$

   _____

   _____

4. Go on a shopping trip and record the prices of the various sources of vitamin C you titrated (orange juice, grapefruit juice, fruit drinks, and tablets). Determine the cost of 60 milligrams of vitamin C from each source. Which source is least expensive? Which source is most expensive?

NOW IT'S YOUR TURN!

1. Design and carry out experiments that will give you data to compare the amount of vitamin C in various packages of orange juice (cartons, cans, fresh-squeezed).

2. Design and carry out experiments to determine the amount of vitamin C in powdered flavored fruit drinks.

   _____

   _____

   _____

3. Determine the amount of vitamin C in the water used to boil a fresh vegetable that is known to be high in vitamin C.

   _____

39 REACTIONS OF BIOMOLECULES

Small-Scale Experiment for text section 27.3

OBJECTIVES

- **Observe** and **record** reactions of important classes of biological molecules.
- **Identify** classes of biological compounds in foods from experimental data.

INTRODUCTION

The food you eat can be classified into five different chemical categories: carbohydrates, proteins, fats, vitamins, and minerals. Carbohydrates are monomers and polymers of aldehydes and ketones with numerous hydroxyl groups attached. One of the simplest carbohydrates is glucose, a monosaccharide, or simple sugar. The chemical structure of glucose looks like this:

Starch is a polysaccharide composed of many repeating glucose subunits. Its structure looks like this:

Proteins are long, continuous chains of simpler molecules called amino acids. Amino acids are compounds containing amino ($-NH_2$) and carboxylic acid ($-COOH$) groups in the same molecule. Linked together, two or more amino acids constitute a peptide. A peptide with more than 100 amino acids is called a protein.

Fats are long-chain carboxylic acids, or esters. Triglycerides are triesters of long-chain fatty acids. The R-groups represent a long saturated or unsaturated hydrocarbon chain.

$$R-\overset{\displaystyle O}{\overset{\displaystyle \|}{C}}-O-R$$

A fat

$$CH_2-OCR$$
$$CH-OCR$$
$$CH_2-OCR$$

A triglyceride

PURPOSE

In this lab you will test various foods for the presence of starch, protein, and fat. You will do this by carrying out some common chemical tests for these kinds of molecules.

SAFETY

- Wear your safety glasses.
- Use full small-scale pipets only for the carefully controlled delivery of liquids.

MATERIALS

Small-scale pipets of the following solutions:

potassium iodide (KI)
starch
water (H_2O)
Sudan III

sodium hypochlorite (NaOCl)
sodium hydroxide (NaOH)
copper(II) sulfate ($CuSO_4$)

Small samples of various foods including: dry cereal, milk, powdered milk, pasta, sugar, potato chips, crackers, peanut butter, margarine, corn oil, yeast, gelatin, and flour.

EQUIPMENT

small-scale reaction surface
scissors
toothpick
white paper

EXPERIMENTAL PAGE

1. To test for starch, mix 1 drop each of KI and NaOCl in each square below with a small sample of the indicated substance. Record your results in Table 39.1.

starch	pasta	cracker	bread	cereal	flour

2. To test for protein, mix 1 drop each of $CuSO_4$ and NaOH in each square below with a small sample of the indicated substance. Record your results in Table 39.2.

milk	powdered milk	yeast	gelatin	bread	water

3. To test for fat, place a small white scrap of paper over each square below, and use a toothpick to stir 1 drop of Sudan III thoroughly with a small sample of the indicated substance. Record your results in Table 39.3.

corn oil	margarine	peanut butter	milk	flour	water

Place this side of the Experimental Page facedown. Use the other side under your small-scale reaction surface.

EXPERIMENTAL DATA

Record your results in Tables 39.1–39.3 or tables like them in your notebook.

Table 39.1   Test for Starch

starch	pasta	cracker	bread	cereal	flour

Table 39.2   Test for Protein

milk	powdered milk	yeast	gelatin	bread	water

Table 39.3   Test for Fat

corn oil	margarine	peanut butter	milk	flour	water

CLEANING UP

Avoid contamination by cleaning up in a way that protects you and your environment. Carefully clean the small-scale reaction surface by absorbing the contents onto a paper towel, wipe it with a damp paper towel, and dry it. Dispose of the paper towels, scraps of paper and toothpicks in the waste bin. Wash your hands thoroughly with soap and water.

QUESTIONS FOR ANALYSIS

Use what you learned in this lab to answer the following questions.

1. Describe a positive test for starch. Which samples gave a positive test for starch?

   _____

   _____

Name _____ Class _____ Date _____

2. Describe a positive test for protein. Which samples gave positive tests?

_____

_____

3. Describe a positive test for fat. Which samples gave positive tests?

_____

_____

_____

4. Which substance contained more than one classification of food?

_____

5. The positive test for starch works because potassium iodide reacts with sodium hypochlorite to produce I_2. The presence of iodine is detected by starch, which turns blue black according to the following unbalanced chemical equations.

____ OCl^- + ____ I^- + ____ $H^+ \rightarrow$ ____ I_2 + ____ H_2O + ____ Cl^-

I_2 + starch $\rightarrow$ blue black starch-iodine complex.

a. Balance the first equation above.

b. Write half-reactions to show the oxidation and the reduction for the first equation above.

_____   _____

6. Sodium hydroxide breaks protein chains into individual amino acids, which bond to copper(II) ions to form a distinguishing deep blue violet color. Draw the structural formula of an amino acid.

7. Sudan III is a fat-soluble dye that imparts a red orange stain to the long-chain fat molecules. Do you expect Sudan III to be very soluble in water? Why?

_____

_____

8. Why do you suppose the dye color of Sudan III intensifies when it is mixed with fats?

_____

NOW IT'S YOUR TURN!

1. Try testing the various foods in this lab for all three classes of biological molecules—starch, protein, and fat.

2. So-called "reducing sugars" have structural properties that will give electrons to copper(II) ion and reduce it.

$$Cu^{2+} + e^- \rightarrow Cu^+$$

Reducing sugars can be identified by using Benedict's solution, which contains copper(II) ions, or Cu^{2+}. When heated, a mixture of Benedict's solution and a reducing sugar turns from blue to green or yellow.

Carry out a positive Benedict's test for reducing sugars in the following way:

a. Combine the chemicals below on a glass slide as shown.

b. Place the glass slide on a hot plate. **Caution:** *The glass will be hot. Handle with a plastic spatula.*

c. Note the change with time. A distinct color change indicates a reducing sugar.

```
2 drops Benedict's solution
          +
     1 drop glucose
```

3. Test 1 drop of various other samples with 2 drops of Benedict's solution. Try H_2O, galactose, milk, honey, etc.

4. Add a drop of HCl to sucrose, a non-reducing sugar. What happens when you add Benedict's solution? What can you conclude?

_____

_____

40 HALF-LIVES AND REACTION RATES

Small-Scale Experiment for text section 28

OBJECTIVES

- **Measure** and **record** the rate at which hydrochloric acid, HCl, reacts with magnesium, Mg.
- **Identify** the half-life of the reaction by interpreting a graph of the experimental data.
- **Determine** the order of the reaction by plotting the experimental data.

INTRODUCTION

A half-life is the time required for one half of the atoms of a radioisotope to emit radiation and to decay to products. After one half-life, half of the radioactive atoms have decayed into atoms of another element. After another half-life, only a quarter of the original sample remains. After another half-life, only an eighth remains, and so on.

Because the concept of half-life is probably unfamiliar to you, you may conclude intuitively that if it takes one hour for half of a radioactive sample to decay, then it should take only another hour for the other half to decay. This conclusion is based on the false assumption that the rate of decay is linear (constant over time). In fact, radioisotopes decay in a nonlinear fashion. The rate of decay slows over time so that the more time has elapsed, the more slowly the decay proceeds. The reactants of many chemical reactions that involve no radioactivity at all react to form products at an easily measurable half-life.

PURPOSE

In this lab you will make a quantitative study of the rate of reaction between hydrochloric acid and magnesium and determine the half-life of the reaction.

$$2HCl + Mg \rightarrow MgCl_2 + H_2(g)$$

As time progresses, the reactants will be consumed. You will stop the reaction after various time intervals by removing the magnesium. You will then measure the amount of HCl consumed in reacting with Mg by titrating the unreacted HCl with potassium hydroxide, KOH. The number of drops of KOH required in the titration is proportional to the amount of HCl consumed by the magnesium. You will then begin the reaction again, stop it after a longer period of time, and titrate the HCl again. By doing this several times, you will have measured the number of drops of KOH required for the titration at various times during the reaction. The same piece of magnesium can be used because the thin ribbon has nearly the same surface area exposed in each run. For this reason the amount of magnesium exposed to the acid in each run will not change. This is important because you will be measuring the disappearance of HCl over time, and you do not want it to be affected by the different sizes of magnesium pieces. Finally, after several runs, the ribbon will become so thin that it will no longer be useful, and you can stop the experiment. You will determine the half-life of the reaction by plotting the drops of KOH used in the titration versus time.

SAFETY

- Wear your safety glasses.
- Use full small-scale pipets only for the carefully controlled delivery of liquids.

MATERIALS

Small-scale pipets of the following solutions:

hydrochloric acid (HCl)

potassium hydroxide (KOH)

phenolphthalein (phen)

water (H_2O)

Solid: magnesium ribbon

EQUIPMENT

watch or clock

EXPERIMENTAL PROCEDURE

1. Add 10 drops of HCl to a clean, dry one-ounce plastic cup.

2. Add 1 drop of phenolphthalein and titrate with KOH, counting the drops to the pink end point. Record your results in Table 40.1 or a table like it. Clean and dry the cup for the next run. Note: This run for time 0 is a titration of the HCl before any magnesium is added.

3. Add 10 more drops of HCl to a clean, dry cup.

4. Cut 3 cm of Mg ribbon. Dip the piece of Mg in a few drops of HCl for a few seconds to dissolve the tarnish. Dry the ribbon.

5. Tilt the cup at an angle and dip the piece of Mg into the HCl for 10 seconds. Hold the Mg ribbon vertically, moving it constantly to dislodge the forming gas bubbles. Keep the magnesium submerged at a constant depth. At the end of 10 seconds, remove the Mg and wash it quickly with water, making sure the wash water enters the HCl in the cup. Dry the Mg for the next run.

6. Add one drop of phenolphthalein and titrate and record your data in Step 2.

7. Repeat Steps 5 and 6 for time intervals of 20, 30, 40, 50, 60, and 70 seconds or until all the magnesium is used up. Record your results in Table 40.1 or a table like it.

Name _____ Class _____ Date _____

EXPERIMENTAL DATA

Record your results in Table 40.1 or a table like it in your notebook.

Table 40.1   Reaction-Rate Data

Run							
Drops of HCl							
Time (s)							
Drops of KOH to pink							
1/drops of KOH							
Log drops of KOH							

1. Calculate the reciprocal of the number of drops of KOH (1/drops of KOH) for each time you measured. Record your results in Table 40.1 above.

2. Calculate the log of the number of drops of KOH, log (drops of KOH), for each time you measured. Record your results in Table 40.1.

3. Make a plot of drops of KOH (*y*-axis) vs. time in seconds (*x*-axis). Drops of KOH vs. time

Drops of KOH vs. Time

1/Drops of KOH

Time (s)

One half-life = 12 sec

CLEANING UP

Avoid contamination by cleaning up in a way that protects you and your environment. Carefully clean the plastic cup by flooding it with water and rinsing its contents down the drain. Shake excess water out, and allow it to dry upside down on a paper towel. Dispose of any remaining magnesium by placing it in the appropriate recycling container. Wash your hands thoroughly with soap and water.

QUESTIONS FOR ANALYSIS

Use what you learned in this lab to answer the following questions.

1. What do you see when Mg reacts with HCl? Write a complete chemical equation and a net ionic equation for the reaction between Mg and HCl.

_____

2. Look at your plot of drops KOH vs. time. What happens to the rate of reaction as time progresses? Why?

_____

3. How many drops of KOH were required to titrate the HCl after 0 seconds? What is half this value?

_____

4. Using your plot of drops KOH vs. time, determine the half-life of the reaction. To do this, find the time required for the HCl to drop to half its value by finding the time that corresponds to half the number of drops of KOH in Question 3.

_____

5. Find the time required for the number of drops to fall to one-fourth of the original value and one-eighth of the original value. Explain how these values also represent the half-life of the reaction.

_____

_____

6. Use your data in Table 40.1 to make the following plots:

   a. 1/drops of KOH vs. time in seconds

b. log (drops KOH) vs. time in seconds.

7. The "order" of the reaction gives us information about the number of hydrogen ions involved up to and including the rate-determining step. The rate of a zero-order reaction is independent of the concentration of HCl. In a first-order reaction, the rate varies directly with the concentration of HCl. The rate of a second-order reaction varies with the square of the concentration of HCl. The order of the reaction of HCl and Mg with respect to the HCl concentration can be determined from the plot that most closely resembles a straight line.

Straight-Line Plot	Order of Reaction
drops KOH vs. time	zero order
log (drops KOH) vs. time	first order
1/drops KOH vs. time	second order

What is the "order" of the reaction with respect to the HCl concentration? How do you know?

_____

8. The rate law for the reaction takes the form: rate = k[HCl]^n where n = the order of the reaction. What is the rate law for this reaction?

_____

NOW IT'S YOUR TURN!

1. Design and carry out a similar experiment for the reaction of $CaCO_3(s)$ + HCl.

2. Design and carry out an experiment to measure the rate of reaction in a different way. For example, measure the amount of hydrogen gas produced over time or the weight loss of magnesium over time.